SECRETS OF ANSWERED PRAYER

SECRETS OF ANSWERED PRAYER

BY

Lester Sumrall

THOMAS NELSON PUBLISHERS
Nashville • Camden • New York

Published in Nashville, Tennessee, by Thomas Nelson, Inc. and distributed in Canada by Lawson Falle, Ltd., Cambridge, Ontario.

Printed in the United States of America.

NOTE: Selected Scripture quotations in this publication have been italicized for emphasis.

Library of Congress Cataloging in Publication Data

Sumrall, Lester.
Secrets of answered prayer.

1. Prayer. I. Title.
BV210.2.S86 1985 248.3'2 85-287
ISBN 0-8407-5925-8

Contents

Introduction

Throughout the ages God's great men have always manifested unusual qualities. Their worldly station mattered little, because the aura of God seemed to surround as many of "low degree" as those of so-called "high degree." Whoever they were, their lives were permeated by the presence of God. Their spoken words were redolent with the odor of God: *God's peace, God's power, God's love*. Their very attitudes seemed His. Their thoughts seemed to come from the heart of God Himself.

How could this be?

Is it true, as some believe, that God has actually chosen some to be great and others to be little, that some should be weak and some strong?

If the answer to the above questions is yes, there would seem to be very little, if anything, that could be done to improve one's station in life or relationship with God.

But if the answer to the above questions is no, then it's logical to assume that some key, some formula, some recipe would enable any believer to plumb the depths and secrets of God, to discover the way to operate within God's plans, and to move with confidence and power.

That's what this book is all about...

It's about that secret recipe, that secret formula, that will enable you to receive from God.

The heart and soul of this book is prayer—the secrets

of prayer. But even more specifically, this book is focused on the secrets of *answered prayer*.

Literally speaking, these are not true secrets, because they are open and available to anybody who desires them. But they are secrets in the sense that they are known and practiced by so few. It is my earnest desire that you will read and appropriate these secrets for yourself.

Personally, I know that prayer works. I know it because I first discovered it at my mother's knee.

I learned that prayer works when I was hopelessly ill and cried out to God. The prayer I prayed that day brought healing to my body. But it also brought great healing to my attitude toward God, toward my fellow men, and toward life itself.

As I have traveled the world, preaching from jungle to arctic and the great reaches between, I have learned for myself that prayer works.

But, I have learned more than that.

I have learned *how* prayer works. I have discovered for myself the secrets of answered prayer.

Those secrets of prayer have wrought miracles in my life, my home, my church, and my ministry. Those prayer secrets have bound demons and set people free. Those secrets have released millions of dollars for the kingdom of God.

And those secrets are yours for the asking.

Jesus Himself provided us with the basic formula to all the secrets of prayer. "Ask," He said, "and it will be given to you;" "seek," He promised, "and you will find"; "knock," He assured us, "and it will be opened to you" (Matt. 7:7).

But, it's more than just asking and seeking and knocking that gets God's attention. It's how and when and in what attitude you do these things. Through the chapters of this book—from years of learning how myself—I reveal to you the secrets of how you, too, can get God's ear and speak to His heart in such a way that when you ask, it will be given you and when you seek, you will find.

So, my friend, I challenge you to turn the pages of this book very slowly, with your Bible and writing materials in hand. Meditate on what you read. *Underline* when a new thought or idea comes to you. Discuss new concepts with your friends and family.

But don't stop there.

Put these secrets to work for you.

Because what you are about to delve into is a vast, practically untapped reservoir of life and power.

1

The World's Greatest Untapped Resource

Prayer is not something you merely think or talk about. Prayer is something you do—God's power made available to mankind, a great resource. Yet, for the most part, prayer is not properly used, not properly "exploited."

Why is that so? Because there is a mystique, a secret, that seems to have placed effective prayer beyond the reach of most believers.

But the power resources of prayer are attainable. Prayer is a force to be used, a tool to be utilized, a mighty weapon to be deployed. This becomes clear and plain as we read: "Finally, my brethren, be strong in the Lord [or, *in Jehovah*] and in the power of His might. Put on the whole armor of God [that's what prayer will teach you to do], that you may be able to stand against the wiles of the devil" (Eph. 6:10–11).

One little known fact God desires to make plain is that it is possible to stand against the tricks of the devil, but to do so, you must certainly learn the secrets of prayer.

"The weapons of our warfare are not carnal but mighty in God for pulling down strongholds" (2 Cor. 10:4). Our weapons are not physical or mental; they are spiritual. One of the best of our weapons is prayer.

Untapped Resources

The earth is replete with untapped natural resources.

Entire oil fields are as yet undiscovered, therefore, untapped. The potential power in that oil does no good until it is discovered and utilized. Untapped diamond fields and rich veins of gold represent almost unlimited purchasing power.

While my family and I were living in the Philippines, the Japanese located and raised an old vessel that had been sunk there during World War II. The vessel was still loaded with coal, which the Japanese simply unloaded on the shores.

In the vessel at the bottom of the harbor, that coal was useless. But when it was brought to the surface and shoveled onto the beaches, it suddenly became a valuable power resource. I watched as hundreds of mothers and children came with baskets and bags and hauled that coal to their homes, where that *potential* power became *actual* power as it was used for heating and cooking.

Prayer is an infinitely more effective energy source than coal. It is the key to the greatest supply of untapped power in the universe. But for the most part, that resource of strength and power is not being used.

Prayer Power in Action

On more than one occasion Jesus' disciples witnessed a demonstration of prayer power. "And when they [the disciples] had prayed, the place where they were assembled together was shaken; and they were all filled with the Holy Spirit, and they spoke the word of God with boldness" (Acts 4:31).

Here are the conditions: the believers *assembled* together and *prayed*. Here are the results: The place was shaken; they were filled with the power of the Holy

Spirit; then they spoke the Word of God—not with backwardness nor fear—with great boldness. First they prayed, then the power came.

If we can get the church in our land to reach out to God through prayer, we will discover resources of strength, blessing, anointing, goodness, and mercies we never dreamed about. If we can convince the world that it is prayer time in our land, the result will be an anointing of power previously unknown.

There are battles that can be won only when we pray. Victories—even over demonic forces—can be ours through prayer.

Let's Get Our People to Pray!

Effective prayer is truly a secret to most Christians. Prayer for the majority of believers amounts only to "Good morning, Jesus," "We thank You for the food," and, at day's end, "Good night, Lord"—all done in two minutes or less. This is not what I am talking about.

I am suggesting that we use prayer as it was designed and intended, as a tremendous force, a terrible weapon against the enemy. I am talking of prayer that can exert a world-changing influence. When it is truly understood and faithfully used, prayer is the greatest source of untapped energy the world has ever known.

To bring about such prayer requires a change in our thinking and in our praying habits. Such prayer among the people of God can change the church of Jesus Christ in America and all around the world. It matters not if you are reading this book in the United States, or in the Philippines, or in Japan, or in South America. Whoever you are, wherever you live, I am assuring you that by your prayers you can receive and set into motion the power of God. Only through prayer is this possible.

United Prayer Produces United Results

Cornelius learned this when he prayed. Cornelius was "a devout man, and one who feared God *with all his household*" (Acts 10:2). Praying together as a family multiplies your prayer power. God tells us that one can chase a thousand, and two can put ten thousand to flight (see Deut. 32:30). As Cornelius learned, when you unite your home in prayer, you become like an army ready for battle. Prayer can change a person, but it can also change entire families!

When Cornelius and his family prayed unitedly, God performed miracles. He sent for Peter, who was one hundred miles away in the city of Joppa. Peter came and preached to Cornelius, resulting in that man's entire family receiving the infilling of the Holy Spirit.

None of these things happened haphazardly. They came about through prayer.

Just as prayer changed Cornelius's life and the lives of his family, prayer can change your life and the lives of those around you. By learning the secrets of prayer, as Cornelius did, you could also be remembered as a person who changed this world and the world to come. Prayer is that powerful!

Prayer Releases Dynamic Energy

You can help others by your prayers. The apostle Paul spoke of this dimension of prayer: "You also helping together in prayer for us, that thanks may be given by many persons on our behalf for the gift granted to us through many" (2 Cor. 1:11).

You see, you can become a prayer partner; you can join with others and become a means of "helping together in prayer." Cornelius helped his family through prayer. You can do the same. You can bless others; you can help missionaries; you can help your pastor and the people of your church; you can help the people in your community and government. All of this and much, much more can be accomplished through your unselfish praying.

You can literally release prisoners by praying. When Herod imprisoned Peter, "constant prayer was offered to God for him by the church" (Acts 12:5). God responded by sending an angel to release Peter. That's the kind of power that's still available to God's people through their prayers! That's the same power that you and your prayer group can have.

Prayer Can Bring Healing

Prayer with faith is also a mighty tool God has given us for physical healing. The Old Testament has many illustrations of God's healing power. For example, Naaman, the great Syrian soldier, was cured of leprosy (see 2 Kings 5:1–14). Hezekiah, king of Judah, prayed to God on his deathbed, and the Lord granted him fifteen more years of life (see 2 Kings 20:1–11). The New Testament provides even more evidence of God's healing power. The Gospels are full of Jesus' healing miracles.

The miracles of healing did not stop with Jesus' return to heaven, either. The book of Acts is full of them too. What most people don't realize is that such healings are a part of the fulfillment of the Great Commission. In that famous command, Jesus said, "Go into all the world and preach the gospel to every creature.... And these signs will follow those who believe" (Mark 16:15, 17). Then follows a list of signs, and included among them is "they will lay hands on the sick, and they will recover" (Mark 16:18).

But the most exciting part of all this for us today is that God can still heal, and He is willing to do so in response to prayer. Jesus told His disciples, "Most assuredly, I say to you, he who believes in Me, the works that I do he will do also; and greater works than these he will do, because I go to My Father" (John 14:12). In the area of healing is this passage: "Is anyone among you sick? Let him call for the elders of the church, and let them pray over him, anointing him with oil in the name of the Lord. And the prayer of faith will save the sick, and the Lord will raise him up. And if he has committed sins, he will be forgiven" (James 5:14–15).

I know from experience that God continues to heal in response to prayers offered in faith. I have seen it happen in my own life. And in my ministry over the years, I have seen hundreds healed through prayer. As a result of these experiences, coupled with the teaching of God's Word, I know that divine healing is both available and effective.

In Whose Name Should We Pray?

God's Word answers this question for us. Jesus said, "And whatever you ask *in My name*, that will I do, that the Father may be glorified in the Son" (John 14:13). That means that the scope of our praying is as limitless as the name of Jesus. Jesus has no limitations, no horizons.

The breadth, the extent, of our praying is as large as our asking. God expects us to reach out to the farthest horizons we can imagine, and to use all the strength and all the power that He has made available to us—all of it in Jesus' name.

So you can see, prayer is not just the mere recitation of words. Prayer is a relationship—with God and with Jesus, His Son. Prayer is the speaking of loving words, a love lyric to our Lord and Savior Jesus Christ.

Prayer is a personal connection with God. Prayer is alive. Prayer is inspiring. Prayer is powerful, energizing, dynamic! Prayer revitalizes the one who prays. But prayer is not just spiritual recreation. As we said earlier, prayer is doing battle with the invisible forces of darkness.

"No man ever prayed without learning something," Emerson said. And he was right. You learn about yourself when you pray. You learn about your fellow man when you pray. You learn about God when you pray.

Prayer Is a Way of Life

A life that is planned and developed by prayer becomes a great life. Prayer puts an indelible stamp upon every thought, every action, of the one who makes it a vital part of his life. The inevitable result of making prayer a way of life is the change of one's very being, the reshaping of his personality into the shape of God.

The power of prayer is as real as the unseen—but also very real—terrestrial gravity, the force with which everyone contends every hour of the day. No one can deny the existence or power of that force. Prayer is a sort of spiritual gravity, spiritual magnetism. Even as a magnet draws iron particles to itself, so God draws people to Himself. And when, through the dynamism of prayer, we turn to God, we find that He responds to us as we respond to Him.

The miraculous power of this spiritual magnetism is evident in every person, in every human body. Dr. Alexis Carrel, a scientist who has seen God's power at work in his patients, and the famous author of *Man, the Unknown*, stated in a *Reader's Digest* article: "As a physician, I have seen men, after all of the therapy failed, lifted out of disease and melancholy by the serene effort of prayer."

The power of prayer is nothing short of amazing. It is the only power in the universe that seems to overcome the so-called laws of nature.

Prayer Is Invincible

Prayer is invincible. It cannot be subdued. Nobody can hinder or prevent the operation of prayer power. Rulers of great nations have had their laws and decrees defied and altered by prayer.

The evil leaders in Babylonia influenced King Darius to defy the power of prayer by casting Daniel into the lion's den (see Dan. 6:10–23). Daniel was unscathed—living proof of the invincible power of prayer.

Wicked Haman learned—too late—the invincible power of prayer. His clever manipulations served only to hang him upon his own gallows, the one he built for his enemy (see Esther 7:10).

It has always been so.

Prayer can destroy enemy powers and evil forces. Prayer can build the kingdom of God. This has always been God's intent.

Prayer operates in the lives of those who have provided God with clean, righteous vessels, in which His Holy Spirit dwells, in which egotism and self-sufficiency have been eradicated. It is in such lives—in which material things have faded and the spiritual life is in proper focus—that God chooses to display His unlimited power.

Evil, self-aggrandizing forces rule the world we live in—political and economic forces, power-hungry forces that are humanly irresistible, immovable, indomitable, insurmountable, impregnable, unconquerable, and unyielding. Yet all these forces are but "paper tigers" in the face of anointed prayer.

Before World War II, France believed its Maginot Line invincible. Germany proved it wrong by simply going around the ends. Germany believed its blitzkrieg manner of warfare was invincible. Yet it was to learn that its "best" would succumb to a superior force.

Our enemy believes himself to be invincible.

Yet when you and I discover the secrets of and appropriate the inestimably superior powers of prayer—the truly invincible "whole armor of God" (Eph. 6:13), the defensive and offensive glories of prayer—we will move into prayer against the enemies of God, the enemies of righteousness, with an assurance, with a joyous abandon, and with an effectiveness we have never known.

When faced with such divine power, all earthly powers are subject to defeat. *All* earthly powers, whether political, economic, or military, are subject to the power of prayer.

Prayer has no equal. The power of prayer does not change. It stands when all other powers fail. World systems change; ideologies change; balances of world power change; balances of economics change. But the power of prayer that is available to us, the power that streams from the Almighty, the Maker of heaven and earth, will never fail. It cannot be defeated.

My friend, the secrets of prayer can be yours. And when you discover them, they will fill you with living energy. You will indeed be able to "mount up with wings like eagles,/...and not faint" (Isa. 40:31).

If you have read this far, the secrets of prayer are already being revealed to you.

2

Definitions of Prayer

Jesus "spoke a parable to them, that men always ought to pray and not lose heart" (Luke 18:1).

In this Scripture Jesus exhorted the people to pray, no matter what the need, the problem, or the sorrow. He advised them to persevere until the answer came. Jesus Himself advocated prayer, but what did He mean? When all is said and done, what is prayer? What does the word mean? If we are to understand the secrets of prayer, we must first understand what prayer is.

Prayer Is the Turning of the Human Soul to God

In this chapter on defining prayer, despite all the other definitions I will use, the basic definiton, the bottom line, always remains the same: Prayer is the turning of the human soul to the living God. Think about that for a moment.

David declared, "To You, O LORD,/I lift up my soul" (Ps. 25:1). In its initial aspects, prayer is the turning of the human personality, the human mind upward toward God.

There might be times of prayer when the lips do not utter words—prayer can be an inward thought. Depending on circumstances, this reaching out to God might amount to a painful wrenching of the heart, an inarticulate moan or groan. God will accept any or all of these as prayer.

When one truly prays he doesn't lift up his heart to saints, to denominations, or to people, but to God. Prayer is the turning of the immortal spirit of man toward the Mighty Creator of the universe. Prayer, then, is communion with God.

Prayer Is Communion with God

"O You who hear prayer,/To You all flesh will come" (Ps. 65:2). Prayer is a communing between your spirit and the Great Spirit of the Universe, which is the Living God.

Adam communed with God "in the cool of the day" (Gen. 3:8), in the Garden of Eden. The two of them communicated with each other. *Fellowship* is another word for communing or communication. When you are in fellowship with another person, you are keeping the lines of communication open.

So prayer is relating to and communing with God. When you are in a position to commune with God, you do not fear Him. You don't approach Him to accuse Him, but to love Him through fellowship with Him. This communion, this communication, this fellowship with God, is prayer.

Prayer Is a Heart Study

Prayer is a heart study because, in prayer, your heart is revealed to you as God sees it. Prayer is a school in which we learn truth that's not available anywhere else. When I don't have the answer to a problem or issue which arises, instead of wasting a lot of time worrying, I pray. As I pray, God reveals to me the decision or the answer to the situation that I need.

Often God reveals myself to me as I pray. A case in point is when I have said something to my wife about a matter. I might think that what I have said is all right, but as I pray, the Lord might say to me, "You spoke too harshly. Your voice carried an edge to it. You were too upset inside and it showed. You should ask forgiveness."

If God does not reveal the incident to me, I might not do anything about it. But when God shows me my heart, my attitude, I can go immediately and ask my wife's forgiveness.

Prayer Is Intensive Desire

Prayer is an intensive desire to see something happen or come to pass; it may be a desire that God has placed within you. That's what the Word of God tells us: "Likewise the Spirit also helps in our weaknesses. For *we do not know what we should pray for as we ought*, but the Spirit Himself makes intercession for us with groanings which cannot be uttered" (Rom. 8:26).

Isn't that beautiful? The Spirit, God's own Spirit, the Holy Spirit, is interceding for us—for me, for you. If you are looking for the will of God, you can find it in prayer, even when you may not be able to find it in thought. But by the intensive desire of the spirit within you, reaching up to the mighty Spirit of God, His will can be made plain to you.

Prayer Is a Spiritual Compass

All ships and airplanes carry compasses, which are vital pieces of navigational equipment. Among their several functions, compasses enable pilots and navigators to know their direction of travel and to pinpoint their exact position at any time. In one of my flights in a small airplane, the pilot pointed to a small town below us and said, "I think that's our destination." But when he consulted his compass, he realized we were about fifteen miles off our course. It was not the town we were seeking.

Prayer is to the Christian what a compass is to a navigator. Prayer will pinpoint our spiritual integrity and show us our weaknesses. Prayer will clarify our positional relationship with God. Even as a compass points the navigator to the North Pole, prayer always points us to our heavenly Father.

Prayer is the most powerful force in the universe. And when a Christian begins to realize the importance, the wonder, the excitement, and the effectiveness of prayer, he will no more divest himself of his regular daily prayer than a navigator would set out on a flight or trip without his compass.

Prayer Is Working with God

Through the divine medium of prayer we can reach right out of our human element to God Himself. This truth is implicit in the prophet Isaiah's words: "He saw that there was no man,/And wondered that there was no intercessor;/Therefore His own arm brought salvation for Him;/And His own righteousness, it sustained Him" (Isa. 59:16).

God was seeking an intercessor to pray. God is still seeking intercessors, men and women (as well as youth) who will commit themselves to intercessory prayer.

That means that you and I are prospects for this critically important work of God's—the work of interceding for His people.

It's exciting to realize that you and I can actually share in the work God is doing in our world.

If you are elderly and can't get out much, you can still be an integral part of God's kingdom. By accepting this opportunity you can proudly say, "I am God's personal assistant. I assist God through prayer."

The prophet spoke of God's cry: "I looked, but there was no one to help;/And I wondered/That there was no one to uphold;/Therefore My own arm brought salvation for Me;/And My own fury, it sustained Me" (Isa. 63:5). God sought men to "uphold," to stand for Him, to stand with Him, to be intercessors; but "there was no one to uphold."

Not only do you and I need prayer in our own behalf, but we have an obligation to pray for God's work in the world; that is, to pray in His behalf. You and I are God's hands. We are His voice. We are His witnesses. We are His intercessors. So when we pray, we are working with God.

" 'So I sought for a man among them,' " God said, speaking through the prophet Ezekiel, " 'who would make a wall, and stand in the gap before Me on behalf of the land, that I should not destroy it; but I found no one' " (Ezek. 22:30).

Here again, God needed someone to stand in the gap. Someone to pray. But apparently He sought in vain—there was no one to labor with Him. I know something of how He felt. There have been times in my life when I was faced with a gigantic task to perform, something that was greater than I could handle. And I looked around for someone to stand with me, beside me, but there seemed to be nobody—nobody at all.

At such times I felt like I was standing alone against a whole battalion of enemy soldiers.

Such a position should never come to a Christian. God tells us to pray for one another. When we help a brother in prayer, we help God's cause, because we are standing with God against the enemy of our souls.

Join with me in telling God, "Lord, You won't ever have to stand alone again. I will stand in the gap with You!"

Prayer Is Divine Reverence

If we are to be effective in our prayer, we must come before our Father in divine reverence. In today's world, it seems that irreverence is the order of the day. Around us we see irreverence for our country, for our flag, for our leaders, even for God Himself. If we are to become mighty in prayer, we cannot allow a spirit of irreverence to overtake us.

Jesus said, " 'But the hour is coming, and now is, when the true worshipers will worship the Father in spirit and in truth; for the Father is seeking such to worship Him' " (John 4:23). In order to pray effectively, one must "worship the Father in spirit and truth." One must have the right spirit when he prays. And that right spirit must be one of respect and honor and deep reverence.

All of the great men and women of prayer I have ever known or read about have been those with whom prayer was serious business. There was no frivolity, no lightness, no joking about this matter of approaching the

King of the universe.

If you desire to learn the secrets of prayer and become a man or woman of prayer, you must learn to reverence the One to whom you direct your petitions.

Prayer Is Divine Obedience

Before you read the rest of this chapter, pause and ask yourself, "Do I harbor a spirit of disobedience within me?"

Are you in a spirit of rebellion against your parents?

Are you in a spirit of disobedience toward God?

Are you in rebellion against the laws of our land?

You must ask yourself these questions, because if you are in a state of rebellion, you cannot receive from God what you desire. The opposite is also true. "Beloved, if our heart does not condemn us, we have confidence toward God. And whatever we ask we receive from Him, because we keep His commandments and do those things that are pleasing in His sight" (1 John 3:21–22).

In other words, obedience is related to success in prayer. If we cannot come before God in humble obedience to His divine will, which is expressed in His Word, we cannot expect to receive His miracles. "And this is His commandment: that we should believe on the name of His Son Jesus Christ and love one another, as He gave us commandment" (1 John 3:23).

If you are to see the manifestations of His power in your circumstances, you must obey Him. You must come to the place where you will speak to Him and say something like this, "Lord, I am being obedient to You in everything I know to do. And I want You to know that I'll do anything You want me to do."

By making such a commitment, you will find yourself well on the way to getting your prayers answered.

Prayer Is the Power That Unlocks God's Treasures

Prayer is the key, the force, the energy, the power that unlocks heaven's treasures and makes them available on the earth.

Some people need healing, but don't pray for it. "Why should I pray? God knows I need to be healed." It's true; God does know you need to be healed. But He has given you the key that will unlock heaven's healing power for you. That power is prayer. Jesus told us, "Ask, and it will be given to you" (Matt. 7:7). Ask. *Pray.*

Need doesn't unlock God's treasures. Prayer does; faith does; intercession does. If you will come to God with the right spirit, using the right keys, you will see God move in your behalf as you have never seen Him move before.

Prayer Is the First Step in Knowing the Lord Jesus

"For 'whoever calls upon the name of the LORD shall be saved' " (Rom. 10:13). The first step in knowing the Lord Jesus is meeting Him in prayer, saying to Him, "Lord Jesus, come into my heart. I am sorry for my sins. Cleanse me from all unrighteousness. Make me a child of God."

Through that beginning you get to know Jesus. You get to know God. You open and begin to receive the treasures of heaven. The whole transaction begins—and continues—through prayer.

Definitions of Prayer

Prayer is very simple, yet, at the same time, very complex. I have outlined and described a few definitions of prayer. Read them until you understand them. Then begin to pray according to God's Word and He will give you the victory you seek.

3

The Laws That Govern Prayer

The Scriptures make it clear that praying is not just hit-or-miss. If a person is going to pray to be heard and to be answered, he must follow certain guidelines.

Jesus outlined some of those guidelines for us in the Sermon on the Mount. " 'In this manner, therefore, pray:/ Our Father in heaven,/Hallowed be Your name' " (Matt. 6:9). " 'In this manner,' " Jesus said; then He set up a proper formula for addressing our Father. When we recognize that fact, and pray in accordance with God's laws or rules concerning prayer, then we will certainly learn how to pray effectively.

The Law of Believing

The first law is the law of believing. Prayers of doubt or fear will not, indeed cannot, be strong prayers. This is true because of the laws of faith that relate to prayer. "But without faith it is impossible to please Him, for he who comes to God must believe that He is, and that He is a rewarder of those who diligently seek Him" (Heb. 11:6). This law states that you must believe that God exists as a powerful, sovereign Lord. This law further states that you must believe that God will answer you ("is a rewarder") when you pray.

If you can comply with both requirements, then you can pray, "Father, I know You are all-powerful, and that You will respond to Your children when they call upon You." When heathen discuss their gods, they may say,

"This god is the god of the hills. This is what he can do..." Or, "This god is the god of the valleys. This is what he can do..."

But we've got the God who is God of everything. He made the whole earth—the entire universe. So when we pray to the One who created everything, we know we are focusing our prayers upon the One with the ability to produce the needed results. We can pray in the confident assurance that He possesses the power to meet any need.

So when we have confidence in Him, our prayers to Him in Jesus' name will not be in vain. They will be answered.

When Elijah confronted the 450 false priests of Baal upon Mount Carmel, he proposed a test. The priests of Baal were to prepare an altar of sacrifice, as was Elijah. Then each was to pray. Elijah challenged the Baalite priests to " 'call on the name of your gods, and I will call on the name of the LORD; and the God who answers by fire, He is God' " (1 Kings 18:24).

The Baalites' idol failed to answer them. Elijah's God answered his prayer by sending fire from heaven to consume the sacrifice.

If you have been born again you have already experienced a miracle in prayer. You can say, "I know God answers prayer because He saved my soul when I prayed. And He delivered me from my sinful habits." Knowing the miraculous power of God in your life enables you to pray with the confident intensity that will make your prayers effective.

The Law of Sincerity

Insincere people don't get their prayers answered, because they are living a lie. The heathen can't get their prayers answered. I have watched the heathen worship in a haphazard manner that indicates insincerity. Even if they knew who God was they could not receive from Him because their lives are built on the shifting sands of lies, falsehoods, artificiality, and deceit.

When one prays sincerely, all facades are stripped away, all deceit is gone and the heart is laid open before God—in total sincerity, with an open spirit, with all hatred gone. There is no other way to approach our God of love. He loves the whole world, and He will forgive the whole world—if only it will come to Him in sincerity.

The law of sincerity is: Anyone in a place of total sincerity before God will discover a blessedness beyond anything he had hitherto dreamed. But there is a cost involved—the cost of commitment, of time.

A minute of prayer here and a minute there—not praying today, if I feel like it, then forgetting to pray tomorrow—is not done in sincerity. And God cannot do great things in the life of such a person. But when the set laws of praying are discovered, practiced, and adhered to, the results will change your life!

The time to begin praying is not when you are in trouble as so many people do (I call that "foxhole praying."). If you pray when things are right, God will come to your rescue when you are in trouble. I can guarantee it.

The Law of Perseverance

Daniel prayed for three weeks to receive the understanding of a vision before the answer came. *Three weeks*! Would he have received the answer if he'd stopped on the fifteenth day? Or even the twentieth day? Of course not. But Daniel stuck to it; he prayed until the answer came. He persevered.

When Elijah prayed for rain on Mount Carmel, he prayed seven times. And each time he sent his servant to see if there were signs of rain. When the servant came back the first time he said, " 'There is nothing.' And seven times [Elijah] said, 'Go again.' " (1 Kings 18:43). What if he had stopped at four times? Or five times? Or even six times? There would have been no rain and the drought would have continued.

Some say, "But Elijah was different. Elijah was a prophet. I can't expect the same victories as Elijah." What does the Bible say about that? "Elijah was a man with a nature like ours, and he prayed earnestly that it would not rain; and it did not rain on the land for three years and six months. And he prayed again, and the heaven gave rain" (James 5:17–18).

You see, Elijah was a man of flesh and blood like you and me. But Elijah knew the law of perseverance. And he held on until the victory came—total, blessed victory.

I'll even venture to say that Elijah may have gotten tired of praying those five, six, or seven times. He probably didn't even feel like praying. Most people pray only when they feel like it. But that's not the time to pray. You don't pray by feelings, but according to needs. You pray when you know in your spirit that it's time to pray, even if in your body you don't feel like praying.

That's when you persist in prayer and your needs are met.

The cities of Sodom and Gomorrah were in trouble because of their wickedness, and God was making plans to destroy them. Abraham interceded for the cities and, incidentally, for his nephew Lot. " 'Suppose there were fifty righteous within the city; would You also destroy the place?' " (Gen. 18:24).

"And the LORD said, 'If I find in Sodom fifty righteous within the city, then I will spare all the place for their sakes' " (Gen. 18:26).

Then Abraham asked, " 'Suppose there were five less than the fifty?' " (Gen. 18:28).

God said, " 'If I find there forty-five, I will not destroy it' " (Gen. 18:28).

Abraham interceded with God until He agreed not to destroy the city if there were as few as ten righteous to be found there. Abraham was persistent in prayer! Have you ever wondered why Abraham stopped with the number ten? Abraham knew that there were ten members in Lot's family, and he thought these ten were righteous.

Abraham hadn't allowed for the fact that Lot's children had intermarried with the Sodomites and become sinners and mockers of God. And even though Abraham saw by the smoke rising over Sodom the next morning that God had destroyed the city, he realized that it could *only* have happened because God had not found ten righteous people in the city. Abraham had persisted in prayer, and God had responded.

The Law of Humility

There are undoubtedly times and places when pride is in order—but not when one prays. Prayer will not be effective unless one approaches the Almighty in humility. Many people pray because they have a need—because they have met with some problem or deficiency in themselves, their family, their community, or their world.

When this realization comes, that person must reach outside of himself to a higher force, a greater energy. So he reaches upward to God and says, "Father, I need Your help."

A self-sufficient person will find it difficult to pray, because he has told himself and others, "I can take care of myself. I don't need anybody. I don't need God." Certainly this person will not receive anything from God.

But there is another kind of pride that prevents answers to prayers. This is the self-righteous person. Have you ever heard anyone pray, "Lord, I have lived for You for forty years. I have taught Sunday school. I've been a deacon. I've given lots of money to the church." And on the basis of his service record he expects to receive blessings from God.

God can't hear the prayers of pride-filled persons. Prayers that are answered come from those who humble themselves before God. God says, " 'If My people who are called by My name will humble themselves, and pray...' " (2 Chron. 7:14).

Those who pray in humility will receive from God. Jesus said, " 'Blessed are the poor in spirit,/For theirs is the kingdom of heaven" (Matt. 5:3). The one who comes to God with praise will receive from God. The ones who admit their need for God and His help will receive from Him.

The truly humble are those who turn to God in the good times as well as the bad. They are the people who touch God's loving heart. And they are the ones who will receive from Him.

The Law of Prayer Structure

The way we structure our prayers is important. And I am not referring necessarily to grammar and syntax, or even to the language we use when we pray. God hears and understands them all. But if we are to pray effective prayers it is important to formulate our prayers properly. Let me explain.

Our prayers should exalt or glorify God. Our prayers should begin with God. Jesus said, " 'In this manner, therefore, pray:/Our Father in heaven,/Hallowed by Your name' " (Matt. 6:9). Such a prayer beginning speaks of one's relationship to the Almighty—"Our Father." It speaks of God's dwelling place—"in heaven." Also, the knowledge of and the acceptance of God's holiness is articulated. In other words, by opening our prayers as Jesus taught, our thoughts are immediately reminded of the divine nature of the One to whom we are directing our petitions. This is important.

Our prayers should usher the participant into the intimate, personal presence of the Almighty. Jesus stated: " 'When you pray, go into your room' " (Matt. 6:6). Whether He meant our bedrooms or merely a special place is beside the point. The point is that both the time and place of prayer should enable one to be apart from worldy, secular things long enough to make it possible for him to be with God and, thus, to commune with Him without interruption.

If one is to pray effectively it is necessary for him to shut out the world, distractions, everything and everybody, so he can become intimate with the Father. A room with a closed door could be that place. A quiet spot in the woods could be that place. Wherever you can be alone with God for a time is a good place.

Daniel knew God better when he met God regularly in a special place. Jacob knew God better when he had wrestled with Him all night. You can know God better when you seek Him on a regular basis, after travailing with Him, being with Him long enough, consistently enough, and deeply enough to become one with Him. It is then that you will become the kind of child of God He desires you to be. It is then that your prayers will be answered. *Our prayers will convince the unbeliever of God's reality and will often bring revival.* Elijah defeated the prophets of Baal and convinced the people of God's reality—when he prayed. The people of Israel turned back to God because of Elijah's praying. Furthermore, these successes in prayer taught Elijah to pray in ways that he hadn't known before.

God is no respecter of persons. He loves you and me as much as He loved Daniel and Elijah. And when we recognize the laws that govern prayer, when we learn how to approach God correctly, bringing our needs to Him in humility and with praise, our prayers will be answered and our faith will be built up.

Let's learn how to pray.

4

The Dimensions of Prayer

The scope of prayer is hidden to millions. Yet, by ripping off the mystical covering in which prayer has been wrapped for centuries, we can discover its secrets. For instance, the mighty agency of prayer can span the globe.

You can approach the Father's throne. You can participate in life-changing acts of mercy and healing. You can change your own life with prayer. You can influence your family and associates by praying. You can participate in the healing of your land by consistent, persistent praying.

" 'If My people...will...pray,' " God said, " 'I will...heal their land' " (2 Chron. 7:14).

In the last chapter, we looked at some important basic attitudes toward prayer that are keys to seeing your prayers answered. Now we want to consider some of the crucial specific elements, or dimensions, of prayer.

The First Dimension Is Confession

"If we confess our sins, He is faithful and just to forgive us our sins" (1 John 1:9). "Confess your trespasses to one another" (James 5:16), wrote James, the earthly brother of our Lord. There is power in confession. Confession initiates a relationship with our Lord. Continual confession leads to growing intimacy with the Most High God. It is through confession that we cleanse our temples, our beings, our minds, our souls, and our spirits of sin and uncleanness.

In one of his timeless appeals to his heavenly Father, David cried out, "Have mercy upon me, O God,/According to Your lovingkindness;/According unto the multitude of Your tender mercies,/Blot out my transgressions" (Ps. 51:1).

The power of this first dimension of prayer is the honest speaking out to God in the *first person*; the admitting to God of who you are; the admission of your *personal* need for Him, your need of His love, your need of His cleansing and forgiveness. It's important to be open and transparent with God, to hold nothing back from Him, to be totally sincere.

The Second Dimension Is Thanksgiving

In today's America most people live better than kings lived two thousand years ago. Even kings did not have at their disposal the food selections we have available in almost any supermarket of the land. They owned no refrigerators. Ice had to be rushed from the distant mountains by a slave, often at the cost of his life. Even homes of Americans who are not wealthy can boast of effective heating in the winter and air conditioning in the summer. And the majority of Americans drive a car of some kind. None of these advantages was available to even the richest of men during Jesus' day.

Yet many Americans are afflicted with the sin of ingratitude. Today's people often have more and appreciate it less than any other generation in the history of mankind. As a general rule they are a thankless, grumbling lot.

Children don't thank their parents for their tender, loving care. In today's world by the time a child is grown, through college, married, and with a home, he may have cost his parents close to a million dollars. That includes hospital costs, doctor and dental care, clothes, education, transportion, music lessons, summer camps, vacations, and more.

How wonderful it would be if children would say to their parents each day, "Thank you, Father. Thank you, Mother. Thank you for all you have done for me"; then go out into the community to thank the grocer, the banker, the police officers, the pastor, and all who have had a hand in their care and welfare; then, above all, thank God for His love and care.

David said, "Oh, give thanks to the LORD, for He is good!/For His mercy endures forever" (Ps. 107:1). It's true; His mercy *does* endure forever.

Smith Wigglesworth, a friend of mine, told me of an incident that occurred while he was in Sydney, Australia. One Sunday afternoon as he was eating dinner by himself in a very large restaurant, he noticed that nobody was praying over his food. So when Mr. Wigglesworth's food was delivered, he tapped his knife on his glass. When he got the people's attention and everybody stopped eating, he stood up and spoke.

"Pardon me, ladies and gentlemen," he began, "but I noticed that none of you as far as I could see have prayed and thanked God for your food. So, if you don't mind, please bow your heads, and I will pray over our food for all of us." Then he prayed.

When he finished and sat down, the restaurant patrons gave him a resounding hand of applause. In addition to being thankful for their food that day, a number of people remained behind to pray and find Jesus as their Savior—all because one man was thankful for God's work in his own life.

Be thankful to God, my friends, be thankful. Whether at home or in a public place, don't begin your meal without pausing to thank God. And while you're at it, don't just thank God for the food, thank Him also for the clothing and shelter He provides. Thank Him for your life, for the air you breathe, for health and strength. Thank Him for every good and perfect gift He provides.

Thank Him also for vast possibilities of a life lived in the Spirit, for a life of prayer.

The Third Dimension Is Worship

In the common vernacular, worship could be considered "courtship" with God—courting His presence, courting His love. It's a terrible blight upon the world when so many people use God's name in vain. Even many Christians blatantly preface many sentences with "God" and "My God." Others frankly curse life, situations, and even their fellow men by damning them in the name of God.

Many others seldom think or speak of God (or to God) unless they are in trouble. Then they beg, "O God, I need You to help me. I need something." It's as though they consider God an eternal Santa Claus.

God cannot be approached casually. He is the Almighty, the Maker of heaven and earth. He must be approached with deep respect, with reverence, adoration, praise, and with worship.

Read the Old Testament example of approaching God in this manner. "Indeed it came to pass, when the trumpeters and singers were as one, to make one sound to be heard in praising and thanking the LORD, and when they lifted up their voice with the trumpets and cymbals and instruments of music, and praised the LORD, saying: 'For He is good,/For His mercy endures forever' " (2 Chron. 5:13).

It is good to tell God He is good.

"The house, the house of the LORD, was filled with a cloud, so that the priests could not continue ministering because of the cloud; for the glory of the LORD filled the house of God" (2 Chron. 5:13–14).

What a sight that must have been! "The house...was filled with a cloud." The glory, the brilliance and majesty, the *shekinah,* the very presence of the Almighty responded to the praise of God's thankful people. God responded to His people's praise in those days. God responds to praise today.

When a person loves God he will praise Him.

Praise is the prayer of thanksgiving—the instrument that will court and nurture an ongoing growth and deep relationship with the Father. Praise is not optional. It is mandatory if one is to maintain a loving, courting dialogue with God.

The Fourth Dimension is Meditation

What, exactly, is meditation? Webster terms meditation as "deep continued thought, deep reflection on sacred matters." In simple terms, meditation in its best sense is the contemplation of God. It is thinking about God, about His Word, about the depth and extent of His goodness. It is waiting upon God.

The psalmist sang, "My soul, wait silently for God

alone,/ For my expectation is from Him" (Ps. 62:5).

"Wait...for God."

A waitress in a restaurant "waits" upon customers by *attending to their needs*. We wait upon God by attending to His needs. What needs, you might ask, does God have? He needs us to think about Him, to glory in His presence, to bask in His Word, to talk to Him, to be with Him for such extended times that we begin to think like Him, and even to reflect the image of His son, Jesus. What a glorious thought!

"But we all, with unveiled face, beholding as in a mirror the glory of the Lord, are being transformed into the same image from glory to glory" (2 Cor. 3:18).

The "Alpine glow" helped me to understand the miracle of this Scripture. The first time I saw the late afternoon sun strike the Alps, transforming them from shimmering white to effulgent gold, I could hardly contain myself. I had never seen such a majestic sight. My thoughts turned to the even greater majesty of my heavenly Father and my Lord Jesus Christ, and I was lifted into the very throne room of the Most High through meditational praise.

The Fifth Dimension Is Petition

Jesus told us, " 'Ask, and it will be given to you' " (Matt. 7:7). We receive from God because we make our needs known to Him. We have been talking about the dimensions of prayer, which include the ways and means of praying. God is looking to us right now, eagerly awaiting the calls, the petitions, the prayers of His children. And when those petitions come to Him according to the formula laid down in God's Word, then He answers them and supplies our need from the bounty of His storehouse.

If you are a clean vessel, a committed child of God, living and growing in His Word and will, and if the need is great enough, and you petition God with unyielding faith, you can expect God to answer your prayers as He did those of Elijah.

Just don't give up. Never give up.

When you pray with the understanding that prayer is the crying out to God with your entire being, that it is the supplication of your innermost person, and that these strong, sincere cryings and petitions are offered to the One to whom your life is totally given, then the Master of the universe will respond and answer your cry.

Even our Lord Jesus understood and prayed according to this principle. "Who, in the days of His flesh, when He had offered up prayers and supplications, with vehement cries and tears to Him who was able to save Him from death, and was heard" (Heb. 5:7).

We must be specific when we pray to our Father. Come to Him boldly (see Heb. 4:16), unashamedly. Tell Him what you need. Talk to Him about those needs. Be consistent in your praying. Write those needs down and present them to Him the next day, and the next, and the next, if necessary.

God loves and responds to persistence and consistency. If you are really sincere with God and go after what you need in the proper manner, I can assure you that you will receive it.

The Sixth Dimension Is Intercession

Children understand the art of intercession. They

know how to hold on until they receive what they want from their parents, whether it's a new bicycle, a new dress, or an ice cream cone. They persist in their intercession with their earthly parents until their requests bear fruit.

Jesus admonished His disciples to bear fruit (see John 15:1–8)—not just a little fruit, but much fruit. And if the vines (Jesus' disciples) don't bear fruit, He promises to prune them until they do (see v.2).

The fruit that Jesus expects can come only by abiding in Him. Without Him we can do nothing of value in the Kingdom. As I minister in many places in the world, I often come across frustrated, unhappy Christians. They find themselves in a mode of defeat for one basic reason—they are unfruitful.

Fruit-bearing comes by intercession. Intercession opens the door of God's abundant storehouse. Intercessory prayer is the praying that won't give up. When there's a need in your life, in your own family, in your church, or in your community, you bear fruit—meet or supply the need in any or all of those areas—by interceding with the Father.

The prayer of intercession is one of the greatest needs of the church today. The prayer of intercession will move mountains. It can change families, communities, and governments.

There are glorious bonuses for prayer intercessors. As you experience the unleashing of God's unlimited power through intercession, you will also experience His unspeakable joy. Because you will have learned how to literally open heaven's doors, you will see your own needs met. You will also see the needs of those around you met as you intercede for them.

Jesus did not command His disciples to bear fruit and leave them hanging, wondering how to go about it. He told them, " 'If you abide in Me, and My words abide in you, you will ask what you desire, and it shall be done for you' " (John 15:7). During the same discourse, Jesus told them, " 'You did not choose Me, but I chose you and appointed you that you should go and bear fruit, and that your fruit should remain, that whatever you ask the Father in My name He may give you' " (John 15:16).

Intercession is beseeching God on behalf of others. Intercession is bearing the fruit. And abiding in Jesus empowers one to intercede in such a way as to bear the fruit.

The Seventh Dimension of Prayer is Travail

Travailing is like prevailing. *Travail,* according to Webster, is "very hard work; toil; labor pains; pains of childbirth; intense pain; agony." Travailing is giving birth. A mother travails in labor and brings forth a new child into the world.

The pain experienced by a woman in labor is unlike any other pain known to mankind and is only dulled by the strongest anesthetic. But the joy of creation, of bringing forth this child into the world, actually transcends her pain.

For the Christian, travailing is wrestling with God for victory. It is believing in something with such passion that no exertion, however difficult or painful, is too great to bring the vision, the goal, the dream, into fruition, or to see bondage removed or a burden lifted.

Travail may result in weeping before the Lord. It may

result in the compassionate agonizing for the release and birthing of souls into the Kingdom.

A mother in childbirth may often feel she is on the brink of death before she delivers. To travail is to be willing to die for a cause. The exertion could be so intense that one may truly be convinced one *is* dying before the answer comes forth. Jesus prevailed in prayer until the sweat drops that fell from His body became great drops of blood. That, my brother, is travailing.

Travail in Prayer Brings Divine Energy

When one travails in prayer to the point of reaching his own outer limits of strength, one experiences a sort of divine energy that enables him to hold on. Spurgeon said, "God does not hear us because of the length of our prayer, but because of the sincerity of it. Prayer is not to be measured by the yard, nor weighed by the pound. It is the might and force of it—the truth and reality of it—the energy and the intensity of it."

Travail Is the Depth of Desire in Prayer

Our Lord Jesus, the Master of all prayer, said, "Whatever things you ask when you pray, believe that you receive them, and you will have them" (Mark 11:24). The word *desire* can be relative. I may desire to see my family saved and do nothing about it. On the other hand, I may so deeply desire to see my family saved that I will travail for hours and days in prayer for them. Jesus was speaking of the travailing kind of desire as being the depth of desire that brings results in prayer.

One can be assured, on the foundation of God's Word,

that those prayers that are meant with one's whole heart and soul, and are prayed with believing intensity, will be heard and answered. And it is such prayers that will change the world.

5

Jesus' Model Prayer

The greatest prayer ever prayed by the greatest Person who ever lived is a powerful prayer. That prayer, usually referred to as the Lord's Prayer, is actually the "Disciples' Prayer." It's the prayer Jesus taught His disciples in response to their request, " 'Lord, teach us to pray' " (Luke 11:1).

This is the prayer He taught them: " 'Our Father in heaven,/Hallowed be Your Name./Your kingdom come./Your will be done/On earth as it is in heaven./Give us day by day our daily bread./And forgive us our sins,/For we also forgive everyone who is indebted to us./And do not lead us into temptation,/But deliver us from the evil one' " (Luke 11:2–4).

Jesus' disciples knew it was difficult to learn how to pray effectively. So it was no wonder that they asked Jesus to teach them to pray. The book of Acts and history bear record that they learned well from Jesus. In fact they learned how to pray so well that they saw the gospel reach out to the extremities of the known world in its transforming power. And when we learn to pray in the manner Jesus taught His disciples, we too will see our prayers answered in a mighty way.

Jesus Had a Wonderful Concept of God as His Father

It was because of His wonderful concept of God as His Father that Jesus prayed as He did, beginning His model prayer with the words, "Our Father." So powerfully has this principle been engraved upon our minds that even today most believers begin their prayers with those reverential words.

Jesus always exalted and magnified His Father. Several examples of this exaltation appear in His great high-priestly prayer: " 'I have glorified You on the earth. I have finished the work which You have given Me to do. . . . That they all may be one, as You, Father, are in Me, and I in You; that they also may be one in Us, that the world may believe that You sent Me.' " (John 17:4, 21).

The only way the world will be able to see and believe in Jesus as the Son of God, the Savior of mankind, is for them to see us, blending ourselves together with God in prayer. It is only when they view us as one with the Father that they will believe in and receive Jesus as their Savior.

In His exaltation of His Father, Jesus truly reverenced His Father's name: " 'I have declared to them Your name, and will declare it, that the love with which You loved Me may be in them, and I in them' " (John 17:26).

How wonderful to know that prayer brings us into sonship with the almighty God. He is not our Father until we call upon Him. However, when we do call upon God and receive Jesus into our lives, we are born again, and truly become children of God. Jesus made it clear that only those who do this are the children of God. And on one occasion Jesus charged a group of people, who were living presumptuously, with the strong accusation: " 'You are of your father the devil' " (John 8:44). The privilege of knowing God as our Father is precious and inestimable.

Jesus Saw a New Kingdom Relationship in Prayer

" 'Our Father,' " Jesus began His model prayer, " 'in heaven' " (Luke 11:2). Then He taught His followers that the kingdom of God is not something far away, but that it's as near as their concept of God. " 'For indeed, the kingdom of God is within you' " (Luke 17:21).

God is interested in what goes on inside of you far more than He is interested in anything else. The new kingdom relationship in prayer demands that God must be enthroned in our heart.

"But what does it say? 'The word is near you, even in your mouth and *in your heart*' (that is, the word of faith which we preach): that if you confess with your mouth the Lord Jesus and believe *in your heart* that God has raised Him from the dead, you will be saved. For *with the heart* one believes to righteousness, and with the mouth confession is made to salvation" (Rom. 10:8–10).

By crowning Jesus King of kings in every aspect of our lives, we recognize and give homage to God, the Father, above all.

When Pilate questioned Jesus and asked Him, " 'Are You a king then?' Jesus answered, 'You say rightly that I am a king. For this cause I was born, and for this cause I have come into the world, that I should bear witness to the truth. Everyone who is of the truth hears My voice' " (John 18:37).

Jesus, who flatly states that His very purpose was to become king, is the One who tells us to address God as, "Our Father, in heaven." And when we do so, we acknowledge the supremacy of the kingdom of God.

Jesus Taught Us to Honor God's Name

Jesus, our Lord, taught His disciples (including us) to hallow, to respect, to give honor to God's name. His name is not to be used or taken lightly. It is not to be used in oaths, which are blasphemous. God's name is sacred and holy. He is the Almighty, the Creator of heaven and earth. He is the One who made us in His own image. He is the One who upholds the earth. Our very breath comes from Him.

Jesus' respect for God's name was traditional among His people. In fact, for centuries religious Jews (especially the orthodox) have refrained from the use of God's name in either speaking or writing. When speaking of the Almighty, they would use a euphemism such as *Ha-Shem* (the Name), or *Ha-Shemyim* (the heavens). And when writing God's name, they would not complete the word, writing it "G-d," leaving out the vowel. Jesus emphasized the importance of the Father's name, and in His model prayer declared that God's name should be remembered as holy.

In His Model Prayer, Jesus Spoke of the Kingdom

He taught His disciples to anticipate the total coming of the Father's kingdom, to look forward to the day when all men would be a part of that grand and glorious rulership. Then after He had prayed, " 'Your kingdom come,' " Jesus went a step further. " 'Your will be done/On earth as it is in heaven' " (Matt. 6:10).

Jesus knew that the will of God is perfectly, scrupulously done in heaven. So in teaching His disciples how to pray, Jesus taught them to desire—and to speak of the desire—that God's will be done here below as perfectly and completely as it is done in heaven. Of course, that should certainly be our prayer today: that God's will be done in our lives—not man's sinful will, not Satan's will, but God's perfect, lovely will.

To paraphrase Jesus' words, it seems to me that He was suggesting that his disciples think, *Lord, in all of my daily thoughts and actions, my strong desire is to do Your will. So, as I approach You in prayer, I ask You to help me to totally perform Your will.* Thus, by constantly thinking of and praying that God's will be done in our lives, our actions will automatically begin to bear out that desire.

Jesus Taught His Disciples to Pray for Daily Bread

Of course, Jesus was not necessarily speaking of physical bread alone, though He doubtless had that in mind when He said, " 'Give us this day our daily bread' " (Matt. 6:11). Basically Jesus was teaching submission to our Lord in everything, every day. This includes believing in God to supply our every need.

Later in this same sixth chapter of Matthew, Jesus said, " 'Seek first the kingdom of God and His righteousness, and all these things shall be added to you' " (v. 33). So, according to Jesus, it is not wrong for us to say, "Lord, today I ask You to supply my necessities, because I am continually putting the things of the kingdom first in my life."

Jesus Taught Divine Forgiveness in This Model Prayer

" 'And forgive us our debts,/As we forgive our debtors,' " Jesus prayed in Matthew 6:12. Jesus taught that divine forgiveness comes through prayer. But forgiveness does not come merely for the asking. Forgiving others is the acid test. We will be forgiven in the same manner, and to the same degree, that we forgive others. In other words, if we do not forgive others, we will not be forgiven. But if we forgive others, we, in turn, will be forgiven. Think about that for a moment.

There can be no resentments, no evil thinking about others, Jesus said. " 'A good man out of the good treasure of his heart brings forth good; and an evil man out of the evil treasure of his heart brings forth evil. For out of the abundance of the heart his mouth speaks' " (Luke 6:45).

Forgiveness is reciprocal. When and as I forgive, I will be forgiven. But if my heart is full of bitterness toward another, I will be unable to forgive him. And if I do not forgive my brother, then God cannot forgive me. Jesus is teaching in this model prayer that we will be forgiven if and when we forgive.

Temptation

" 'And do not lead us into temptation' " (Matt. 6:13). There are those who teach that God tempts some of His children. This is a false teaching. "Let no one say when he is tempted, 'I am tempted by God'; for God cannot be tempted by evil, nor does He Himself tempt anyone" (James 1:13). Praise the Lord for His concern for His children! God is our Helper, not our tempter. God loves to strengthen us, to build us up. The devil is the one who desires to hurt us and lead us astray. For that reason Jesus calls the devil a thief.

Jesus said, " 'The thief does not come except to

steal, and to kill, and to destroy. I have come that they [My children, My disciples, My followers] may have life, and that they may have it more abundantly' " (John 10:10).

Jesus knows the heart of His Father. He knows how God loves us and that He "will not allow you to be tempted beyond what you are able, but with the temptation will also make the way of escape, that you may be able to bear it" (1 Cor. 10:13).

" 'But deliver us from the evil one' " (Matt. 6:13). Whenever evil presents itself, God always provides a way out. There is no evil in the world from which God cannot deliver you if you are doing what He has called you to do. But if you are dabbling in sin, you've got a problem.

In essence, Jesus is saying in this model prayer, "The Father and I can deliver you from any evil, no matter what it is." And if you, even right now as you read, realize that you are bound by any sin and any evil thing, I want you to know that you can be delivered from it here and now and begin walking in freedom and power.

Jesus Had a Vision of World Dominion in Prayer

" 'For Yours is the kingdom and the power and the glory forever' " (Matt. 6:13). Jesus realized the totality of the Father's kingdom. He knew better than anyone else that God is the source of all power and that to Him all glory is due. For that reason, He incorporated these words into this prayer for His disciples. As believers, we need to be continually reminded of who we are: that we are the sheep of His pasture, and that all our strength and power flow from the Lord God.

The apostle Peter echoed Jesus' words when he wrote, "To Him be the glory and the dominion forever and ever. Amen" (1 Pet. 5:11). The psalmist sang, "Give unto the LORD,/O you mighty ones,/Give unto the LORD/glory and strength" (Ps. 29:1).

These strong affirmations should be a part of every believer's prayer life. Awareness of our Father's kingdom and power and glory, and our constant remembrance of them will help us build a strong relationship with our heavenly Father. For all of us who love Him are His children, and all of us are equal in His sight. And He is the almighty God. He is the Creator of the universe. He is our Holy God.

" 'Our Father in heaven.' " *My* heavenly Father.

" 'Hallowed be Your name.' " I will give unto God the glory due His name. And I will not forget to praise Him.

" 'Your kingdom come.' " I will live in continual anticipation of Your kingdom rule.

" 'Your will be done.' " No longer my will, my desires—only what He desires in my life, on earth, as in heaven.

" 'Give us this day.' " Not next year's need, not even next week's need, but today's—I will depend upon the Lord today.

" 'Forgive us.' " I will forgive others—regardless of what they have done—in order that You, Lord, will forgive me.

" 'And do not lead us into temptation.' " Instead lead all of us, Lord, so we will not stumble or stray from the pathway.

" 'Deliver us.' " Deliver us from all evil. I thank You

for Your great salvation, which is for all of us, including me.

" 'For Yours is the kingdom and the power and the glory.' " The Kingdom is Yours, Lord. And Your Kingdom is within me. You've got the power. I give You the glory—forever. Thank You, Lord, for making me a part of all that You are.

Forever. Amen

God's Kingdom, God's domain, is everlasting. It is endless. And it is eternally present—forever and ever and ever and ever. Through prayer that is in line with the model prayer that Jesus taught His disciples, we will see His Kingdom come. We will see His Kingdom established throughout all the earth. And we will see every language, every land, every people come under His lordship.

" 'Our Father in heaven,/Hallowed be Your name./ Your kingdom come./Your will be done/...forever. Amen' " (Matt. 6-9, 10, 13).

6

When Jesus Prayed

Jesus was a person of frequent, persistent, prevailing prayer. Prayer was an indispensable part of everything He was. It was the source of His spiritual life, His spiritual growth, His spiritual power. He enjoined His disciples to "Watch and pray, lest you enter into temptation" (Matt. 26:41).

There were at least two pivotal moments in His life when Jesus' prayers stood out above all other times. One was at the Garden of Gethsemane, when Jesus faced the reality of the Cross. Though His disciples had come with Him, Jesus left them to rest, while He went farther into the garden and prayed so intensely that He sweat great drops of blood (see Matt. 26:36–44; Luke 22:44).

A second prayer of monumental importance came during those dark awful hours He spent upon the cross. Though He was undergoing the intense agony of crucifixion, Jesus' heart went out to His tormentors and, on their behalf, He prayed, " 'Father, forgive them, for they do not know what they do' " (Luke 23:34). There is no doubt about it—our Lord was a Man of prayer.

When and Where Did Jesus Pray?

Deep, prevailing prayer is not always convenient. Effective prayer demands a commitment to time and place. Jesus exemplified this fact. "Now in the morning, having risen a long while before daylight, He went out and departed to a solitary place; and there He prayed" (Mark 1:35).

When did Jesus pray? He prayed during the early cool of the day. He prayed when there was no one around, when there were no interruptions. He spent early, quality time with His Father. He prayed while His mind was fresh and unencumbered with the countless details of living. Have you ever risen very early in the morning to pray? I often find those times the most refreshing, the most rewarding, the most precious.

Where did Jesus pray? He could have stayed in His room, or even in the house. But He didn't. He found a solitary place in which to approach and commune with His Father. As our example, Jesus prayed. He prayed frequently. He spent quality time in prayer. He prayed when and where He would not be beset by interruptions.

Though Jesus had come from the Father, He knew wherein His strength lay—in prayer. So, if Jesus needed to pray, how much more must we? If He needed to find quality time to pray, how much more should we? And if He deemed it necessary to get totally away from others while He prayed, shouldn't we?

If you own an automobile, you know you must put fuel in it regularly, or it will quit running. You know you must feed your body regularly, or it will die. Prayer is the fuel that feeds the spirit of man. And if your spirit is not refueled by frequent prayer, it will run down and come to a total stop.

Christ Also Spent Entire Nights in Prayer

"Now it came to pass in those days that He went out to the mountain to pray, and continued all night in prayer to

God" (Luke 6:12). *All night in prayer to God*!

"But I can't do that," people say. "I've got to get my rest." I need my rest, too, yet I have spent many nights in prayer. Then I've had to get up and get going the next day, meeting and counseling with people. I agree, it isn't easy!

But when I have prayed the night through for whatever reason, my spiritual batteries have become fully charged despite my physical weariness. It must have been so with Jesus, because throngs of people often wanted merely to touch Him. How much He must have needed the refillings that came from those nights alone with His Father.

The result was always a fresh supply of power and anointing that was sufficient for the never-ending drain upon His spiritual resources. But during those nights when He prayed, laying before the Father the needs of a hurting, sinful world, God met Him. And our Father will do the same for anyone who cares enough to forfeit a few hours' sleep to rendezvous with the Almighty.

For a man to give up his rest to intercede for others reveals his sincerity. And for a man to devote to God alone a morning, a day, or an entire night reveals his passion to help and bless people and indicates that they are his first concern.

The Church Must Rediscover Its Source of Power

Today's church has beautified itself by constructing great buildings and impressive citadels of worship. But that same church, in many cases, is out of touch with people. As a result, America has produced an entire generation that doesn't know God, that doesn't love and serve Him. My friends, *this generation needs God*!

Today's church must be reborn for the task of reaching this generation for God. It must reach to the mountaintop and spend time in prayer. The church in South Korea has done so and has literally saved the nation. In that land, thousands of people rise at four o'clock every morning and go to the mountaintops to pray. We need the same awakening in America, in all of our land, and in our churches.

We need to seek God. We need to learn how to search for Him with all of our hearts. We need those mountaintop prayer meetings. We need those times of solitary prayer. We need them a thousand times more than Jesus ever did.

Prayer Was Jesus' Communion, His Inspiration, His Strength

Jesus set the prayer pattern for us. He was showing us how to live, how to worship, how to pray. And if we would be successful in our lives for the Lord, we would do well to follow our Lord's example.

Jesus said, "Men [and women as well] always ought to pray and not lose heart" (Luke 18:1). God wants us to learn to pray in times of adversity, in times of turmoil, in times of problems. He wants us to pray and not lose heart or give up. Don't quit. Don't give up. Anybody can do that. But it takes fortitude, courage, and commitment to pray and not lose heart.

Prayer Held No Second Place in Jesus' Life

To me it's beautiful to realize that even though Jesus

was the Son of God, the Savior of the world, prayer was always in first place in His life. Prayer held number one priority for Him. Is prayer in first place in your life? Does it have that same priority in your life as it did in Jesus' life?

Let's be very honest: most of us pray if we have time. We pray if the baby doesn't cry and disturb us. We pray if the neighbors don't come over for the evening. We pray if we don't have to clean the house...or go shopping...or go to work. Isn't that right?

But if prayer is to be effective in each of our lives—as God intended it should be—it has to hold topmost priority in our lives.

When Jesus went to the mountaintop to pray, He was there for that single purpose. Nothing disturbed Him there. So He prayed. And until you and I can learn to utilize prayer in the same single-minded fashion, we'll never be able to reach the mountaintops of blessing and anointing and receive all of God's blessings.

The High-Priestly Prayer of Our Lord

Jesus' prayer in John 17 is one of the greatest chapters in the entire Bible. In it we can feel the very heartbeat of the Master as He prays to His Father. And the concerns for His people that He expressed there are concerns that we should share as we go to God in prayer. Let's look at some of those things Jesus prayed about in His high-priestly prayer, the prayer in which we can also sense the depth of His love for the Father and for us, His children.

Jesus prayed that His disciples would all be one. " 'Now I am no longer in the world, but these are in the world, and I come to You. Holy Father, keep through

Your name those whom You have given Me, that they may be one as We are' " (John 17:11).

What a precious realization—Jesus prayed for you and me! And He prayed that we might be one with Him in the same way that He is one with His Father! Think of the closeness, the warmth, the sharing that goes on between fathers and sons. And Jesus is asking the Creator of the universe to bring about that same affinity between Jesus and all His followers. The fact that Jesus prayed for this indicates that such is possible, and that we should pray for it as well.

Jesus prayed that His disciples would have joy. " 'But now I come to You, and these things I speak in the world, that they may have My joy fulfilled in themselves' " (John 17:13). How wonderful to realize that when Jesus prayed for me (and for all of us), He prayed that we might possess His own divine joy! With Jesus' resources available, we should never be sad or unhappy. We should truly be filled with joy, His joy. And truly, "the joy of the LORD is your strength" (Neh. 8:10). When we are joyful, we are filled with strength. But when our joy is gone, we become weak. This, too, is a proper subject for our prayers.

Jesus prayed that all of His disciples be kept from evil. Jesus knew that all His followers would be under attack. His prayer was: " 'I do not pray that You should take them out of the world, but that You should keep them from the evil one' " (John 17:15). God doesn't take us from our jobs to keep us from exposure to evil. The devil is determined to destroy us and continually tries to draw us away from God and His Word. But Jesus, the Son of God, prayed that we would not be overcome by any of the tricks the devil employs against us, and we need to pray likewise every day.

Jesus prayed that His disciples would live holy lives. " 'Sanctify them by Your truth. Your word is truth' " (John 17:17). "Sanctify them," Jesus prayed. The word *sanctify* simply means to set apart for a sacred purpose, to consecrate, to purify. How are we to be sanctified, set apart, purified? There is only one way, only one means—the Word of God.

God has provided His Word as the instrument of our sanctification. "Christ also loved the church and gave Himself for it, that he might sanctify and cleanse it with the washing of water by the word" (Eph. 5:25–26). We sanctify ourselves by availing ourselves of His resources, by reading the Word of God, by obeying the Word of God, by living as the Word of God directs, and by praying for His purifying to be accomplished in us.

Jesus prayed that His disciples be perfect. "I in them, and You in Me; that they may be made perfect in one, and that the world may know that You have sent Me, and have loved them as You have loved Me" (John 17:23). This is amazing, but it's exactly what Jesus prayed—that we may be made perfect in Him, that the world around us might come to know the love of God in Christ by observing our clean living and our godly lives. Certainly we need to ask God daily to use us as effective witnesses of His love.

Jesus prayed that His disciples would receive eternal life. " 'Father, I desire that they also whom You gave Me may be with Me where I am, that they may behold My glory which You have given Me; for You loved Me before the foundation of the world' " (John 17:24). Think of it; Jesus prayed that the inhabitants of the entire world might receive eternal life.

" 'For God so loved the world that He gave his only begotten Son' " (John 3:16). Jesus is that only begotten Son described in this Scripture. He is the One who prayed for us—for you and me—that we might inherit life everlasting. What a blessed hope we have in Jesus! And in like manner, we should pray daily for the salvation of those we love who do not yet know the Savior.

Whatever we are or become in our spiritual lives, we owe it all to the Savior who gave Himself for us, who *prayed for us* that we might be one with Him, and who gave us such a beautiful pattern to follow in our own prayer lives.

7

How the Holy Spirit Helps Us Pray

The Holy Spirit of God (sometimes called the Holy Ghost because of the King James translation) powerfully helps us when we pray. Jesus also called the Holy Spirit the Comforter and the Spirit of Truth. He taught His disciples that the Comforter would abide with them forever (see John 14:16). The Holy Spirit's continuous presence in our lives enables us to "live in the Spirit" as well as to "walk in the Spirit" (Gal. 5:25).

Living in the Spirit is accomplished by continually feeding on God's Word, by learning to know God in a personal and intimate way, and by patterning our lives after all of His instructions. Living in the Spirit and walking in the Spirit are synonymous terms indicating that one has made himself subject to all of God's will and way in his life. It means whatever God tells me to do I will do. It means pleasing Him is the very first consideration of my life. It means I am seeking the Holy Spirit's guidance in my life, I am depending on His help in my life, and I want Him to direct my life.

One of the ways the Holy Spirit operates in the prayer life of a believer is indicated in Romans 8:26: "Likewise the Spirit also helps in our weaknesses. For we do not know what we should pray for as we ought, but the Spirit Himself makes intercession for us with groanings which cannot be uttered."

"The Spirit helps in our weaknesses." He does this because we often don't know how we should pray about specific situations. Our understanding of what is needed and what is in God's perfect plan may be incomplete. It is at such times that the Holy Spirit makes intercession for us.

"With groanings which cannot be uttered." Often as we pray we are so concerned or burdened with the awareness of a need that our hearts cry out to God with intensity inexpressible by words themselves. The Holy Spirit within us interprets those "groanings," those inarticulate cryings, into words that are understood by God.

We also see the Spirit's help in Ephesians 6:18: "Praying always with all prayer and supplication in the Spirit, being watchful to this end with all perseverance and supplication for all the saints." Praying always means tuning our hearts to God with every heartbeat; every breath, another contact with our Father. Though we will have special times of prayer, praying should become so much a part of us that we will often breathe a prayer without even thinking. The Holy Spirit, ministering to our spirits, makes this possible.

"With all prayer and supplication...being watchful to this end with all perseverance and supplication for all the saints." Casual praying is not effective praying. Prayer is a mighty force. Prayer is capable of changing men and nations. This means that one's prayers must be serious and intense if they are to achieve their intended purpose. Again, the Spirit helps us to pray in this manner.

Times of prayer become especially meaningful, more victorious, and more effective when our praying is done in cooperation with the indwelling Spirit of God. When we learn to do this, praying becomes a natural part of our existence and as much a part of our daily living as eating or sleeping.

Why Should We Pray in the Spirit?

Genuine prayer must come from the spirit of a man, not just from his mind. Your mind consists of your thinking and feeling capacity, and of your decision-making capacity, your will. All of these parts make up your soul and are under sin until you are born again, at which time your spirit comes alive. When your human spirit comes alive, then God's Spirit (the Holy Spirit) can become the King and Controller of your mind, your emotions, and your will. This is where prayer comes in.

Your praying begins with your spirit, then flows into your mind to direct it through your emotions into your will. Thus prayer influences your total soulish nature. This is one reason why prayer is so important to the individual who is doing the praying.

Therefore, when you are born again and learn to live in the Spirit, it means that the indwelling Spirit of God has access through your regenerated human spirit into your mind and will, thus affecting your entire being. Praying in the Spirit, then, indicates that the words that flow from your lips come from your Spirit-dominated and -directed human spirit, and not entirely from your mind.

So you can see the importance of learning to pray in the Spirit. Since you are praying as directed by the Holy Spirit (see Rom. 8:26), you are hooked into the source of all power, the almighty God Himself.

When the spirit and the soul are under the control of

the Holy Spirit, the body will also come into line. This means that the body's five senses will act in accordance with the desires of the Holy Spirit of God.

This results in victorious living, which, in turn, results in victorious, powerfully effective praying. When one reaches this place in his spiritual growth, his feet will go where the Spirit directs; his hands will do what the Spirit desires; and his lips will speak only words that will glorify the living God.

Prayer by the Spirit Conforms to the Bible

God's Word is our guideline, our plumbline. If we always conform to the Word of God, we will never go astray. Error and the cults begin when someone deviates from the clear teaching of the Word of God and says, "God told me something different. He has given me a special revelation." Or, instead of basing his theology, thinking, and actions upon the Word, he says, "I *think* this, or that..."

God's Word is always right and we must line up our lives with it. It doesn't matter what a man may teach. If his teaching is in opposition to God's Word, the man is wrong, not the Bible. If a church or denomination teaches something contrary to the eternal Word of God, it is in error, not the Bible.

This illustrates the importance of praying in the Spirit. If we are in alignment with God's Word, our praying through and by the Spirit of God will be clear and accurate, powerful and effective. You can absolutely count on this truth: God's Word and the Spirit of God will always be in harmony—always. They will never disagree with each other, because the Word of God and the Spirit of God are one. They flow together and are inseparable. The Holy Spirit is described in John 14:17 as " 'the Spirit of truth, whom the world cannot receive, because it neither sees Him nor knows Him; but you know Him, for He dwells with you and will be in you.' "

The two are instruments of love and blessing and power. So when we pray in the Spirit, we pray in the Word of God and by the Word of God and fulfill the Word of God.

Someone recently asked me, "Tell me, how do you judge some new doctrine?"

I said, "It's very simple. You lay it alongside the Word of God and judge it by the whole Bible—not by a verse, but by the entire Bible. If it is rightly related in harmony with the Bible, it's all right, and the Spirit will confirm that fact with your spirit. But if it happens to be somebody's private interpretation, or someone's personal revelation, it will be in disagreement with the Bible at some point. That means it's in error, and the Holy Spirit will make that plain to you. So don't follow it!"

If someone says to me, "If you don't accept my revelation, you are going against God," I don't accept that either.

But I do accept the Word of God—all of it. That's number one. And praying in the Spirit is an integral part of the Word of God, so I accept it, because praying in the Spirit always glorifies God. Always.

Why should we pray in the Spirit? "For what man knows the things of a man except the spirit of the man which is in him? Even so no one knows the things of God except the Spirit of God" (1 Cor. 2:11). There's the answer. We need information about how to pray, but we can know it only through the Spirit of God. The Spirit of

God is the divine Carrier of God's very thinking. And when we know God's thoughts about a subject—particularly about His will for our lives—then we can joyfully, expectantly, happily live and grow in our oneness with Him. We can pray for others with a knowledge we never possessed before.

My friend, if you have never experienced the release, the knowing, the power, the tremendous peace that comes in relating to the Holy Spirit in prayer, I urge you to open yourself up to Him and ask Him to take over your life *and* your prayer life. When you do so, you will wonder how you ever managed to get along before.

8

The Bible Teaches Us the Value of Prayer

If one is to learn about prayer, he must go to the Bible, because the Bible is the key source book for prayer. God's Word is our immovable, unshakable prayer foundation. Prayers that are not founded upon that Word will go amiss and fail. Conversely, all prayers that are properly founded on His Word *will not* fail.

Men who changed the world were men of prayer. Moses was a man of prayer. On at least one occasion he spent forty days and forty nights in prayer. And Moses's leadership had an impact upon the world such as no other man has ever made. Though the Jews call Abraham "our father," only Moses do they call "our teacher." Moses's communion with God in prayer made him what he was. Elijah was also a man of prayer. He also prayed forty days and nights. His life also had a powerful effect upon the world.

In what way does the Bible influence our praying?

The Bible Reveals God's Nature

If we are to have confidence in God, and if we are to believe that we can depend upon Him, we must understand who He is. The Bible tells us who God is and what He is like.

O LORD, our LORD,
How excellent is Your name in all
  the earth,

You who set Your glory above the
heavens!
...When I consider Your heavens,
the work of Your fingers,
The moon and the stars, which You
have ordained,
What is man that You are mindful
of him...? (Ps. 8:1,3–4).

The heavens declare the glory of God;
And the firmament shows His handiwork (Ps. 19:1).

Hundreds of other passages declare the greatness, the majesty, the power, the glory, the extent of our God. If we are to become strong in prayer, we must read those passages. We must know them if we are to know God's nature. And when we know God's nature, we can pray to Him in confidence.

Solomon's great dedicatory prayer of the temple begins with, " 'LORD God of Israel, there is no God in heaven above or on earth below like You, who keep Your covenant and mercy with Your servants who walk before You with all their heart' " (1 Kings 8:23).

Jesus' great teaching prayer for His disciples begins with, " 'Our Father in heaven,/Hallowed be Your name' " (Matt. 6:9). One great prayer of the disciples began with, "LORD, You are God, who made heaven and earth and the sea, and all that is in them' " (Acts 4:24).

All of these prayers had their basis in the Bible, and all of them gave honor to the innate nature of God.

God's Word Is Vital in Prayer

I believe that the Bible in your life will cause your prayer life to abound. By that I mean that an intimate acquaintance with the Word of God will cause you to want to pray; it will actually give birth to your praying. Deep study of the Word of God and frequent involvement with the Word of God will, quite naturally, cause prayer to spring forth from your heart and from your lips.

I first became aware of this truth in the life of my mother. As a child I would often see her praying with her Bible in her lap. She had read until prayer came to her lips; then she put her Bible down and prayed. She taught me that Bible reading and prayer often flow together and become one.

Perhaps you have sometimes knelt and read a chapter or more from your Bible aloud. And you were aware that God had accepted that reading of His Word as prayer—because the reading forth of the Word of God with your lips had actually been a prayer, and God brought forth the desired results of that prayer in your life.

The Bible Causes Prayer to Come Alive

The Bible "is a tree of life to those who take hold of her" (Prov. 3:18); "the Word of God is living and powerful" (Heb. 4:12). Jesus said, " 'The words that I speak to you are spirit, and they are life' " (John 6:63). When the living Word of God becomes an important part of you, its vitality is imparted to you. When this happens, God's Word makes your prayers come alive.

When God's Word is alive in you, things happen when you pray. There are many examples of this in the Bible. For instance, there was Hezekiah, the king of Israel. At one time he was "sick and near death," and he "prayed to the LORD, saying, 'Remember now, O LORD, I pray, how I have walked before You in truth and with a loyal heart, and have done what was good in Your sight' " (2 Kings 20:1–3). God heard Hezekiah's prayer and gave him fifteen more years of life.

As we study this Bible example, we can build up our own faith to pray for a specific need as Hezekiah did. As we pray, our prayers will be prayers of faith, not prayers of doubt. Such prayers become prayers of thrilling expectation, because we have seen in God's Word what He has already done in a particular situation such as ours. When we have confidence in what God has said and what He has done, then we pray boldly and realize what we have asked.

This is the biblical principle behind what I've been saying: "So then faith comes by hearing, and hearing by the word of God" (Rom. 10:17). And then we have God's wonderful promise concerning prayer: "Now this is the confidence that we have in Him, that if we ask anything according to His will, He hears us. And if we know that He hears us, in whatever we ask, we know that we have the petitions that we have asked of Him" (1 John 5:14–15).

Elijah was a man of God, a mighty man of faith. And when the son of a widow whom he knew died, Elijah prayed, " 'O LORD my God, I pray, let this child's soul come back to him.' Then the LORD heard the voice of Elijah; and the soul of the child came back to him, and he revived" (1 Kings 17:21–22).

Prayers like these, rooted firmly in the Word of God, will change your life and the lives of your family. Prayers of faith like these will change the world. As you read the Word of God, do so with your heart open, and your reading can become praying. Likewise, when you pray, have your Bible close at hand. Because, as you have seen, the two of them—God's Word and prayer—flow together. Thus, even as the disciples asked Jesus, "teach us to pray" (Luke 11:1), by your frequent and intimate involvement with God's Word, He will teach you to pray as well.

Faith Is a Key to Prayer

Why is it that some believers are never able to pray strong, effective prayers? One reason may be that they do not spend time studying the Word of God.

As we have just read, the Bible creates faith. If you are not praying in faith, your exposure to God's Word may be limited. This is serious. If you don't pray in faith, your prayers will not be heard; they will be empty, useless, dead.

God's Word, your faith, and your prayer are closely, essentially related. In other words, God's Word in you, building up your faith, will result in answered prayer. The opposite is also true—the lack of God's Word in you, resulting in little or no faith, will lead to few if any of your prayers being answered.

Here's a principle you can count on: God's Word in you in abundance will teach you how to pray effectively.

The Bible Teaches Man How to Listen and Pray

One of the major problems with most Christians is that they talk more than listen. Have you ever watched a group of people in conversation? Try observing them when they don't know you are watching. In most cases, two or more people are talking at the same time, while the others are waiting for a momentary break in the flow of words so they can jump in with their ready contribution.

Hardly any of them are listening!

Too often this happens when we approach God in prayer. We have become so accustomed to talking, talking, talking, without listening, that we pray, pray, pray, without hearing what God is saying to us. Therefore, we don't hear from God. It isn't that He isn't speaking to us. Rather, we don't hear because our ears are so full of the sound of our own wordiness that we can't hear Him. It's a simple, organic fact that nobody can be speaking and listening at the same time. We do one or the other.

As a child, Samuel, who became a mighty man of God, learned a valuable lesson. He was told to say, " 'Speak, LORD, for Your servant hears' " (1 Sam. 3:9). In other words, "I am going to keep still, Lord. I know You are talking to me. So I will listen and keep my mouth shut."

When we develop such an attitude and put it into practice, we will be able to hear from God. But all too often we tell God by our actions, if not by our words, "Listen, God, for Your servant speaks."

No matter how much you think you have to say to God, who is the Creator of the universe, it is never as important as what He would say to you. Prayer has two sides to it—your side and God's. If you have something to say to Him, say it, and listen. If you come before Him to praise Him, do so, and become quiet before Him. If you sense His desire to speak to you, come before Him *and listen.*

If, in your praying, you develop the ability to listen to God, you will be the richer for it.

I have known persons of great prayer power to become quiet before the Lord for long minutes at a time. And their prayers often are not in words, but simply inarticulate groans of great intensity. They were not really speaking; they were listening.

At such times these people were learning from God. I have also learned that God can speak to me most effectively while I listen during times of prayer. Also, I have found that these moments of quiet with God are times when I get to know Him in a much better, more intimate way.

The Bible Teaches Man to Declare War in Prayer

This was true with Jacob when he encountered an angel and wrestled with him in prayer all night. As daylight approached the angel said, " 'Let Me go.' " But [Jacob] said, 'I will not let You go unless You bless me!' " (Gen. 32:26).

And the angel blessed him. He said, " 'Your name shall no longer be called Jacob, but Israel [a prince of God]; for you have struggled with God and with men, and have prevailed' " (Gen. 32:28). Such biblical events can teach you to pray. Such accounts will also show you that prayer is not always easy. Sometimes prayer is difficult because you are fighting, not against flesh and blood, but against principalities and powers of the demonic world. It was against these forces that Daniel fought and prevailed in prayer for twenty-one days (see Dan. 10:1–14).

Elijah fought spiritual warfare in prayer.

Jesus fought spiritual battles in prayer.

Scores of others in the Bible held out against evil

forces in prayer. And all of them are examples that prove to us that *we can fight, and win, spiritual battles* in prayer. Sometimes the fight is difficult, grueling, grinding. But when you hold on—when you fight the good fight of faith, when you pray without ceasing—and win the victory, how sweet that victory is! You, like Jacob, have become a prince, because you have learned something of inestimable value—you now possess power with God.

Then it is that your friends (and enemies, too) will see the shine of victory upon your face. Praise God! You have fought a good fight. And you have won it!

9

Fasting: Another Secret of Answered Prayer

Prayer and fasting are the believer's secret weapons. "Consecrate a fast,/Call a sacred assembly;/Gather the elders/And all the inhabitants of the land/Into the house of the LORD your God,/And cry out to the LORD" (Joel 1:14).

Prayer alone is a powerful force—"The effective, fervent prayer of a righteous man avails much" (James 5:16). But fervent prayer in combination with spiritual fasting comprises an "unbeatable duo" against which all the resources of hell cannot prevail. It must be "spiritual" fasting, because mere physical fasting, for health or to lose weight, does not move God.

But when one becomes so concerned, so burdened over a need, a person, a country, or a problem that he chooses not to eat for a period of time in order to devote himself to prayer, then prayer *with* fasting becomes a power that can shake even the very demons in hell.

Though many fasts are recorded in the Bible, the Bible tells of only three men who fasted for as long as forty days—Moses, Elijah, and Jesus. Each of them fasted for a specific purpose. During their lengthy fasts, each was supernaturally sustained. And at the conclusion of each of these fasts, each person had achieved his spiritual objective.

At a time when a great move of the Spirit of God was needed amongst the people of God, "The word of the LORD...came to Joel....Consecrate a fast,/Call a sacred assembly...and cry out to the LORD" (Joel 1:1,14). God knew the power that would be released when His people would cease eating and all ordinary pursuits—and pray. God knew it and commanded the prophet Joel to proclaim the fast.

Throughout the Bible there are examples of outstanding events that came about when God's people fasted. I will show a few of them. The first is when...

Nations Were Saved through Prayer and Fasting

"And I fell down before the LORD, as at the first, forty days and forty nights; I neither ate bread nor drank water, because of all your sin which you committed in doing wickedly in the sight of the LORD, to provoke Him to anger" (Deut. 9:18). This was a crucial time in Israel's history.

After Moses led the people out of Egypt, they began to murmur, to grumble, to complain. Nothing pleased them. Then they reverted to their former idolatry. At this point God moved to judge them. He expressed His anger to Moses, saying, " 'I have seen this people, and indeed they are a stiff-necked people. Let Me alone, that I may destroy them and blot out their name from under heaven' " (Deut. 9:13–14).

Moses fell down—prostrated himself on his face—before the Lord and prayed. He fasted and prayed for forty days and forty nights, without eating any food or drinking any water. He interceded for the people that God wanted to destroy.

Moses was willing to give his very life for these people. It is a medical fact that one cannot live without water for forty days and nights. Fasts of forty days have been recorded even in modern times. But it is impossible to live without water or liquids for that length of time. So God miraculously sustained Moses while he interceded for the Israelites.

And because of his earnestness, his sincerity, his burdened and broken heart, Moses's prayer was heard by God and He spared the people!

Fasting with prayer can perform miracles for a person. It can perform miracles for a country. Our own country needs many to pray and fast for it right now. Our president has proclaimed days of prayer for our land, and many thousands have prayed. But we haven't seen the miracles we need to see, because those thousands who prayed weren't as desperate as Moses was when he prayed.

Nineveh was also saved by prayer and fasting.

Nineveh was an extremely wicked city to which God had dispatched Jonah to preach. After at first refusing to go, Jonah finally went to the city. He went into the very heart of Ninevah "and cried out and said, 'Yet forty days, and Nineveh shall be overthrown!' " (Jon. 3:4).

Nineveh had a choice. Its people could have chosen to ignore Jonah's cries, or they could have simply ridiculed Jonah and laughed him out of the city. They could even have said, "Well, let's wait and see. If things get bad, then we will do something about it. But let's just see."

Of course, if God had dropped fire upon them as he had Sodom and Gomorrah, there wouldn't have been anything left to wait for. But God was merciful. We read:

> The people of Nineveh believed God, proclaimed a fast, and put on sackcloth, from the greatest to the least of them. Then word came to the king of Nineveh; and he arose from his throne and laid aside his robe, covered himself with sackcloth and sat in ashes. And he

caused it to be proclaimed and published throughout Nineveh by the decree of the king and his nobles, saying, "Let neither man nor beast, herd nor flock, taste anything; do not let them eat, or drink water. But let man and beast be covered with sackcloth, and cry mightily unto God; yes, let every one turn from his evil way and from the violence that is in his hands. Who can tell if God will turn and relent, and turn away from His fierce anger, so that we may not perish?" Then God saw their works, that they turned from their evil way; and God relented from the disaster that He had said He would bring upon them, and He did not do it (Jonah 3:5–10).

Nineveh was a city overrun with sin, a city upon which God had laid His judgment, a city saved by fasting with prayer! Nineveh, one of the great metropolises of that day, was saved from God's fierce anger when its people fasted and prayed.

Could it be that some of your prayers (and mine) are not answered because we have not fasted? Could it be that we have not been sincere enough to forego a few meals to pray? Could it be that the face of our great land might be changed in the same way as Nineveh—through prayer and fasting?

A Major City's Building Project: Directed by Prayer and Fasting

The Israelites had been held captive in Babylon for many years. And when a portion of them returned to Israel, the land had been laid waste. Jerusalem, their beloved city, was in ruin. The buildings had been razed. The walls were broken down and the great wooden gates had been burned. It was a terrible sight to behold.

When word of this utter destruction reached Nehemiah, cupbearer for King Artaxerxes, in Shushan, he was greatly upset. He wrote:

So it was, when I heard these words, that I sat down and wept, and mourned for many days; I was fasting and praying before the God of heaven. And I said: "I pray, LORD God of heaven, O great and awesome God, You who keep Your covenant and mercy with those who love You and observe Your commandments, please let Your ear be attentive and Your eyes open, that You may hear the prayer of Your servant which I pray before You now, day and night, for the children of Israel Your servants, and confess the sins of the children of Israel which we have sinned against You. Both my father's house and I have sinned. We have acted very corruptly against You, and have not kept the commandments, the statutes, nor the ordinances which You commanded Your servant Moses. Remember, I pray, the word that You commanded Your servant Moses, saying, 'If you are unfaithful, I will scatter you among the nations, but if you return to Me, and keep My commandments and do them, though some of you were cast out to the farthest part of the heavens, yet I will gather them from there, and bring them to the place which I have chosen as a dwelling for My name. Now these are Your servants and Your people, whom You have redeemed by Your great power, and by Your strong hand. O Lord, I pray, please let Your ear be attentive to the prayer of Your servant, and to the prayer of Your servants who desire to fear Your name; and let Your servant prosper this day, I pray, and grant him mercy in the sight of this man." For I was the king's cupbearer (Neh. 1:4–11).

Jerusalem was really in a mess. Thousands of people were coming back from their long captivity to inhabit their "wonderful city," and it was in almost total ruin. These people had no place to live and no protection against the roving hordes of enemies who sought to wipe them out. It was a terrible situation.

What happened? Nehemiah and the people prayed and fasted. And God granted them the finances to rebuild the city and provided them with protection while they did so—because people fasted and prayed!

Fasting is hard work. I know. I've fasted on numerous

occasions. And my body doesn't like to fast. Your body doesn't want to fast either, nor do your friends want you to fast, nor does the devil want you to fast. He knows that fasting and prayer unleash the powers of heaven.

Prayer and Fasting Changed a Modern-Day Prison

I remember one Christmas Day when I went to a prison with several large boxes of oranges, apples, and candy to give to the prisoners. After I had sacked it all up and given it out to the inmates, I stood up and spoke to them.

"Ladies and gentlemen," I said, "I refused my Christmas dinner today and left my family at home, just to be with you. Just to tell you that I love you. I want you to have your Christmas, but I don't want any. I preferred to come and be with you—to tell you that you are lost. I came to tell you that Jesus loves you. And I'm going to pray for you..."

As I spoke, the Spirit of the Lord came upon that prison and people began moving toward God. I think everyone in the bullpen where I was preaching was converted. And some prisoners in the other cells got saved too. They came and knelt where we were and began to weep and cry. They made such a racket that the jailers came running downstairs.

"What's happening this Christmas?" they asked.

They saw all the prisoners kneeling and praying, while the others were rejoicing, and they couldn't comprehend it all. "What's happening?" they asked over and over again.

I said to one guard, "Well, about everybody in jail has gotten saved."

Even as I spoke to that jailer, the Spirit of God came upon him and he fell to his knees on the other side of the bars. With tears running down his face, he wept and prayed until God met his heart's needs. It was a marvelous day! And all because of fasting and prayer! I know that if I had not fasted and prayed that prison revival would not have taken place. I know it, because prayer with fasting is a powerful force. I've seen the difference.

Daniel Pierced the Unknown through Prayer and Fasting

The redemption of Israel, including the rebuilding of the temple, was expected but had not yet come. Daniel showed his concern when he said:

> Then I set my face toward the Lord God to make request by prayer and supplications, with fasting....while I was speaking in prayer, the man Gabriel...informed me, and talked with me....In those days I, Daniel, was mourning three full weeks. I ate no pleasant food, no meat or wine came into my mouth, nor did I anoint myself at all (Dan. 9:3; 21–22; 10:2–3).

Daniel was in earnest. His people had been in captivity for seventy years. Even most of those who had come as young children had died, and few remembered their homeland. But a remnant strongly desired to go back to repopulate the land. The promised time for their return had come and passed. Now, as a man of God, Daniel threw his entire being into the spiritual battle to regain Israel for his people. He fasted and prayed for three weeks. It took some time for an answer, but God did answer his petition.

Then, suddenly, a hand touched me, which made me tremble on my knees and on the palms of my hands. And he said to me, "O Daniel, man greatly beloved, understand the words that I speak to you, and stand upright, for I have now been sent to you." . . . Then he said to me, "Do not fear, Daniel, for from the first day that you set your heart to understand, and to humble yourself before your God, your words were heard; and I have come because of your words" (Dan. 10:10–12).

The impasse was broken and the battle was won when a man of God prayed and fasted! Jesus Himself declared that there are some battles in the unseen world that can only be won " 'by prayer and fasting' " (Matt. 17:21). Daniel won his battle with the use of those powerful spiritual weapons.

Witnesses Were Sent Forth When the Church Fasted and Prayed

John Wesley once declared that God doesn't do anything except in response to prayer. That premise might be debatable, but biblical evidence indicates that God does move when effectual, fervent prayer is offered.

It was so in the first-century church. The Word of God was being well received throughout Israel and in the surrounding areas. But there was a need to reach out even further as Jesus Himself had commanded in His Great Commission. But who was the fledgling church to send? The problem was solved in a most interesting manner.

Now in the church that was at Antioch there were certain prophets and teachers: Barnabas, Simeon who was called Niger, Lucius of Cyrene, Manaen who had been brought up with Herod the tetrarch, and Saul. As they ministered to the Lord and fasted, the Holy Spirit said, " 'Now separate to Me Barnabas and Saul for the work to which I have called them.' " Then, having fasted and prayed, and laid hands on them, they sent them away" (Acts 13:1–3).

The biblical method of sending forth prophets and teachers is through prayer and fasting. How many evangelists, pastors, missionaries, and other workers do we anoint and send forth by the same method? If we desire total victory in the Lord, we must do everything according to the pattern laid down in His Word.

Cornelius Received God's Revelation by Prayer and Fasting

For a number of years after the Day of Pentecost the gospel was preached only to the Jews, and very few non-Jews (Gentiles) came into the faith. But God desired the Jews to be a "light to the Gentiles" (Isa. 42:6). How was this to be? It all came about when a certain Gentile prayed and fasted. When, in a totally unprecedented move, Peter came into Cornelius's home to preach the gospel, Peter asked him how it had all come about.

Cornelius answered: " 'Four days ago I was fasting until this hour; and at the ninth hour I prayed in my house...' " (Acts 10:30). The spiritually hungry man prayed and fasted; then God spoke to Peter in a vision, which provided the necessary impetus for Peter's entering an unclean Gentile's home and sharing Jesus Christ with him. Again, prayer and fasting were the key.

Why Should I Fast?

When you fast, you minister to and benefit every portion of your tripartite nature—you strengthen your *spirit;* you bring your *soul* into subjection; you weaken the hold your *body* has on your entire being. The body and its five senses try to dictate to the spirit and soul body. Most of the time it does a pretty good job and we listen to our physical body.

When our body says, "I'm tired, and I don't want to read the Bible. I'm too tired to pray," the undisciplined believer usually allows the body to do about what it wants to do. And when the body says, "I'm hungry. Feed me," we usually do as the body demands. All of this points to the fact that in most believers their bodies' needs transcend the needs of their spirits and souls. But the apostle Paul declared that he determinedly brought his body into subjection (see 1 Cor. 9:27), and urged all believers to follow his example (see 1 Cor. 11:1).

Fasting is one way to bring the body into subjection. Thus, when I strengthen my spirit (in the Word), my spirit begins to talk to my mind, emotions, and will (which make up the soul); and the mind tells the body, "Body, you are *not* in control. You are the slave of your spirit!"

So, basically, fasting enables the believer to gain control of his entire being and to bring himself into a strong, positive, ever-deepening relationship with God. Fasting—gaining control over your body—proves to God that you love Him and that you can put Him first in all things.

That's why, when you are fasting, you are able to focus your entire being upon praying. You deny the body the ability to usurp your attention from the Word of God and the purpose of your praying. So, with all bodily powers brought into line with God and His Word, "the effective, fervent prayer of a righteous man avails much" (James 5:16).

A fasting believer is an effectively praying believer. A fasting church is a strong, growing church. Let's involve ourselves in the exciting business of praying with fasting. It's a dynamic key to spiritual power through answered prayer.

10

What Happened When the Early Church Prayed?

The apostle Peter preached a powerful sermon on the day the church was born. Referring to the mighty outpouring of the Holy Spirit, he said, " 'But this is what was spoken by the prophet Joel' " (Acts 2:16). All of this had been foretold centuries before, Peter told them.

He talked to them of Jesus, whom

> 'God has raised up, of which we are all witnesses. Therefore being exalted to the right hand of God, and having received from the Father the promise of the Holy Spirit, He poured out this which you now see and hear.... Therefore let all the house of Israel know assuredly that God has made this Jesus, whom you [the Jewish leaders] crucified, both Lord and Christ' (Acts 2:32–33, 36).

Those were powerfully anointed words, and when Peter's listeners heard them,

> they were cut to the heart, and said to Peter and the rest of the apostles, 'Men and brethren, what shall we do?' Then Peter said to them, 'Repent, and let every one of you be baptized in the name of Jesus Christ for the remission of sins; and you shall receive the gift of the Holy Spirit. For the promise is to you and to your children, and to all who are afar off, as many as the Lord our God will call.' And with many other words he testified and exhorted them, saying, 'Be saved from this perverse generation.' Then those who gladly received his word were baptized; and that day about three thousand souls were added to them (Acts 2:37–41).

Three thousand souls! What a tremendous ingathering for the Kingdom in that one day on that grand birthday of the church! But that wasn't all. "And they continued steadfastly in the apostles' doctrine and fellowship, in the breaking of bread, and in prayers" (Acts 2:42).

"And in prayers." That became the watchword of the first-century church—prayer. What was the result of all this?

> Then fear came upon every soul, and many wonders and signs were done through the apostles. Now all who believed were together, and had all things in common, and sold their possessions and goods, and divided them among all, as anyone had need. So continuing daily with one accord in the temple, and breaking bread from house to house, they ate their food with gladness and simplicity of heart, praising God and having favor with all the people. And the Lord added to the church daily those who were being saved (Acts 2:43–47).

Jesus had taught His disciples well. He had given them His model prayer. Then He had trained them to go out to teach, to preach, to cast out demons. He had taught them how to pray. And they remembered. After He had taught them for forty days after His resurrection, He told them the Holy Spirit would come upon them in just a few days.

"Now when He had spoken these things, while they watched, He was taken up, and a cloud received Him out of their sight" (Acts 1:9). For the next ten days the disciples prayed with one accord. "These all continued...in prayer" (Acts 1:14). No wonder there was such a harvest of souls during those first few days after the church was born.

Acts of the Apostles/Holy Spirit

That harvest continued. They prayed; God answered.

They prayed; men were healed. They prayed; God sent them unto the uttermost parts of the earth to tell the good news that Jesus was the resurrected Messiah. Throughout the book of Acts (which really should be called the Acts of the Holy Spirit, because of the way the Holy Spirit moved through the lives of those disciples), God honored His word, and miracles happened.

The Acts of the Apostles/Holy Spirit go on, providing a book that will never be finished or closed. Those heroic men and women made church history and provided a model for the present-day church. God did it then. He will do it again, when we learn to pray as they did.

Those early believers "continued steadfastly in the apostles' doctrine and fellowship, in the breaking of bread, and in prayers" (Acts 2:42). They enjoyed the company of other believers. They went to the temple together. They went from house to house sharing the Word and building up each other in the most holy faith. They fellowshipped together. They ate together. They partook of the Lord's Supper together. They listened to the apostles' doctrine together—the teaching, the ministry of the Twelve.

And they prayed together.

Prayer brought predictable results. "Then those who gladly received his word" (Acts 2:41) were a joyful bunch of people, as all believers ought to be. Here's a principle you can count on: Where there's joy in serving the Lord, there will be power. And these people were so joyful and happy that thousands were drawn to hear the message.

The devil often tells prospective believers, "If you become a Christian you won't have any fun. You'll have to wear a long face and be sad all the time." But these are lies. I have discovered that Christians are the happiest people on earth. This was evidently the case as described in this Scripture before us, because joyful, happy believers transmitted their joy to others who then "gladly received" (Acts 2:41) the Good News and became themselves partakers of the faith of Jesus.

This multitude of joyful people was baptized in one day and was added to the growing number of followers of the Messiah!

In my ministry I've seen plenty of sad sinners. I've seen them in jails and prisons, in brothels and mental institutions, in night clubs and in gambling houses. Yes, there is plenty of sadness in the hearts of those who follow the devil.

But those who love the Lord are filled with gladness. "He has put a new song in my mouth—Praise to our God" (Ps. 40:3). And prayer in the early church had a strong place in bringing this new joy and "new song" to pass in others.

Prayer in These New Believers' Decision-Making Process

Many books tell you how to make decisions, but the best decision-making book of all is the Bible, God's Word. These early Christians found it so on numerous occasions. In line with Jesus' instructions, they spent ten days in prayer before the Holy Spirit fell on the Day of Pentecost.

Their decision in selecting Judas' successor was made after prayer (see Acts 1:24). As they met in each others' homes daily, their decisions were directed by prayer. They prayed and praised God for all of His goodness to them in every situation.

The believers spent regular times in prayer each day, with the men praying at the temple three times daily. No doubt Peter's and John's actions in chapter three of Acts were dictated by the Holy Spirit. On that particular day, a great miracle of healing took place when the lame man at the gate begged for money. His healing set in motion a chain of events that resulted in beatings and imprisonments for Peter and John.

Some of the Jewish hierarchy were hard put to suppress the exuberant manner in which these new believers were spreading the gospel of Jesus. After they had imprisoned Peter and John they brought them before the council.

> And they called them and commanded them not to speak at all nor teach in the name of Jesus. But Peter and John answered and said to them, "Whether it is right in the sight of God to listen to you more than to God, you judge. For we cannot but speak the things which we have seen and heard." So when they had further threatened them, they let them go (Acts 4:18–21).

What did Peter and John do then? Did they quail in fear? Did they complain about their hard life? Did they ask, "God, what are You doing to us?" They did none of these things. "And being let go, they went to their own companions and reported all that the chief priests and elders had said to them. So when they heard that, they raised their voice to God with one accord and said: 'Lord, You are God' " (Acts 4:23–24).

How did they decide their next move? They prayed and God directed them to decide to keep right on doing what they were doing.

But wasn't that in defiance of the law?

No. It was in defiance of the decisions of men who were themselves in defiance of God. There is no law higher than God's law. The greatest, fairest, most comprehensive law book in the world is the Bible. The Bible comprises the total law. So when a law is made that is contrary to God's law, believers are not obligated to obey it. This was the disciples' conclusion as they prayed. Then they acted upon the decision that God had helped them to make.

On another occasion, Peter was imprisoned. What were the people to do about it? And how were they to conduct themselves when the life of one of their leaders was in danger? Again, their decision was to pray. And this time, God sent an angel to Peter and delivered him from the guards' hands.

What about your own decision-making? Do you always seek the Lord's guidance before you make decisions? Or do you, as many are prone to do, make a decision, and ask the Lord to bless it and cause it to succeed? God is interested in every decision. Make it a rule of your life to seek His guidance in all your actions—large or small—and you will find your life richer, fuller, and more effective.

In the Early Church, Prayer Led to Praise

Those early believers prayed daily. They prayed in each others' homes. They prayed in the temple. They prayed alone. They prayed together. It seemed they were always praying. And their praying usually led to praise. They did all of this "with one accord...praising God" (Acts 2:46–47).

When Peter and John went to the temple to pray (see Acts 3:1), their time of prayer led to praise when the lame man was healed. Peter and John praised the Lord.

The formerly lame man praised God. The witnesses in the temple praised the Lord. All the believers praised the Lord. The only ones who didn't praise the Lord were the priests, the captain of the temple, and the Sadducees, none of whom were happy with the new faith and power of the believers.

When Peter and John were forbidden to speak in Jesus' name, they went to their people for a prayer meeting. "And when they had prayed, the place where they were assembled together was shaken; and they were all filled with the Holy Spirit, and they spoke the word of God with boldness" (Acts 4:31).

Prayer led to praise. Praise led to bold witnessing with great power. And this witness led again to praise.

Those early believers had no corner on praise. The same principles work today. If you will spend regular time in prayer, you will soon find yourself in praise. It's an automatic chain reaction that always works. If you haven't learned it yet, try it. It will work for you as it did for them.

11

How Many Times Should We Pray for One Thing?

How many times do you think we should pray for something? There are those who declare that once you pray over a matter—either for a soul to be saved, for someone to be healed, for a domestic situation, or for anything—repeating that same prayer indicates unbelief.

Think about that for a moment, because it's very important to understand the ramifications of that position.

Let's restate the question more specifically. If you ask God in prayer to save your son, should you never ask Him again? If you ask God to guide you in a decision, should you never seek guidance in that same situation again? If you ask the Lord to help you solve financial problems, are you never to pray concerning finances again?

I am asked often how many times we should pray for something.

My answer is always, "Let's see what the Word of God has to say concerning your question."

Jesus "spoke a parable to them, that men always ought *to pray*, and not lose heart" (Luke 18:1). The Master Himself epitomized this concept. He prayed continually. And He never lost heart. Since Jesus is our model, we should follow His example.

Remember, as believers, we're involved in spiritual warfare. This is no game, no child's play. And we're not wrestling "against flesh and blood, but against principalities, against powers, against the rulers of the darkness of this age, against spiritual hosts of wickedness in the heavenly places" (Eph. 6:12).

Spiritual Soldiers Fight Until They Win

In a war you fight to win. And, if you're a good soldier, you dig in and fight *until* you win. You don't quit. This same principle applies to spiritual soldiers involved in spiritual warfare. It applies to prayer. You cannot afford to be a quitter in anything, especially in prayer.

You may be involved in a spiritual battle to see someone come to the Lord. So you pray earnestly a time or two, or for a week or a month. If you don't see any progress, you quit. Do you realize that you may have quit just an hour, just a day too soon? And that if you had not lost heart and quit, the victory would have been yours?

I thank God that throughout history there were people who didn't tire of praying. Martin Luther prayed many times before he was able to take a strong, public stand that "the just shall live by faith," and win his spiritual freedom. John Wesley prayed many times before his "heart was strangely warmed" at Aldersgate and the course of his life, as well as the course of his country, was changed. The founders of our country prayed many times before God removed all the barriers and the United States of America became a reality.

Now, back to the opening question: If you pray more than once for anything, is the second prayer a prayer of unbelief?

My answer is a firm, unequivocal no! I cannot accept that theological precept, and I urge you to open the pages of Scripture with me to examine both sides of the question.

We will first examine the account of the Israelite's assault upon an "impregnable" enemy city.

And the LORD said to Joshua: "See! I have given Jericho into your hand, its king, and the mighty men of valor. You shall march around the city, all you men of war; you shall go all around the city once. This you shall do six days. And seven priests shall bear seven trumpets of rams' horns before the ark. But the seventh day you shall march around the city seven times, and the priests shall blow the trumpets. Then it shall come to pass, when they make a long blast with the ram's horn, and when you hear the sound of the trumpet, that all the people shall shout with a great shout; then the wall of the city will fall down flat" (Josh. 6:2–5).

Joshua had sense enough to do exactly what God told him. He didn't argue and ask, "Lord, why should we march more than one time? Why should we pray more than once? Aren't You able to perform a miracle with just one prayer?"

Joshua obeyed God and the people marched. They marched and they prayed. They did it one day; God said, "Do it again." They did it the second day; God said, "Do it again." This action was repeated until God's command was fulfilled to the letter. Then the miracle happened.

They prayed their way around that city thirteen long, weary times before the answer came. But when they obeyed God, He gave them the miracle they sought.

If they had left the Ark (the symbol of God's presence) behind when they marched, the miracle would not have been given them. If they had let the trumpeters remain in camp on the seventh day, the miracle would not have happened. *If they had ceased praying* after the first, or the second, or even the twelfth time, the miracle would not have happened. But they persisted in prayer as

God commanded, and they got their miracle.

Why did God say march around the city once a day for six days, then seven times on the seventh day? I don't know. I only know that when Joshua and the people obeyed God, He gave them a mighty miracle. He gave them the hitherto "impenetrable" city of Jericho. It fell to the Israelites without a fight.

There are reasons for answered prayer. The first and foremost is obedience—strict, absolute obedience. There are also reasons for *unanswered* prayer. The first and foremost is disobedience.

I believe prayer is like the ocean tides. When the tide begins to roll in, the water is low and the beach is covered with flotsam and trash. Then a wave rolls up higher. The next ones come up farther. Soon each successive wave is lapping even higher upon the shore. And as each one pushes its way farther upon the beach it washes away the trash.

Prayer is like the tide. Pray. Pray again. Pray again. Each time you pray, the devil is defeated again. Each time you pray, more is accomplished. More clutter and trash are washed away, and the miracle you desire is closer to realization. Each time you pray for a situation or person, it's like another march around Jericho, or like another wave on the beach. Though you don't see the answer, it is being accomplished!

So you pray till the answer comes. Like the march around Jericho, the city *will* fall down. Like the tide, it will come in.

Elisha's Persistence Resulted in a Miracle of Healing

There was no doubt about it; the child was dead. Elisha's servant reported it to his master. This child was a special child, a child of promise. The Shunammite woman had longed for a child, but her husband was old, and she despaired of having one. Now, just as the prophet had predicted, she had a child. But tragedy had struck. The child had died. She sent for Elisha.

> Elisha...went up and lay on the child, and put his mouth on his mouth, his eyes on his eyes, and his hands on his hands; and he stretched himself out on the child, and the flesh of the child became warm. He returned and walked back and forth in the house, and again went up and stretched himself out on him; then the child sneezed seven times, and the child opened his eyes" (2 Kings 4:34–35).

This is an outstanding miracle of healing that took place because a man of God would not give up easily. He stretched himself out on the child, praying as he did so, several times before the miracle of healing occurred.

He could have given up and buried the child. But he refused to do so. Once was not enough, so he came back and repeated the performance. And the child was brought back to life.

Persistence Brought Healing to Naaman

Naaman was a mighty general of the Syrian army. He had wealth and power. He had everything he needed. But he had something he didn't need—leprosy. And if his leprosy were to be discovered, he would become an outcast. Something had to be done. It was a serious situation.

The Jewish maid of General Naaman's wife suggested that he go to Elisha the prophet. "Elisha will cure you of your leprosy," she promised.

Naaman refused to visit a mere prophet. He presented

himself to the King of Israel with his request. When Elisha heard of the request, he sent a messenger to Naaman telling him to

> 'Go and wash in the Jordan seven times, and your flesh shall be restored to you, and you shall be clean'...So he went down and dipped seven times in the Jordan, according to the saying of the man of God; and his flesh was restored like the flesh of a little child, and he was clean (2 Kings 5:10, 14).

At first Naaman was angry at being sent to the tiny, muddy Jordan River. But he finally went. And you can be sure that with each of his dips in that river he prayed: "God, make me clean. God, make me clean..."

After a dip he was still leprous. But he dipped again.

After the second time under, he checked himself. His skin still bore the marks of the disease.

So he dipped again. And again. Each time he prayed.

God blessed his persistency. And he was healed.

Jesus Taught Persistence in Prayer

"Then He spoke a parable to them, that men always ought to pray and not lose heart" (Luke 18:1). In this parable, Jesus told of a persistent widow who came to the judge again and again with her requests until they were granted.

On one occasion, even Jesus prayed for a blind man twice.

> Then He came to Bethsaida; and they brought a blind man to Him, and begged Him to touch him. So He took the blind man by the hand and led him out of the town. And when He had spit on his eyes and put His hands on him, He asked him if he saw anything. And he looked up and said, "I see men like trees, walking." Then He put

His hands on his eyes again and made him look up. And he was restored and saw everyone clearly (Mark 8:22–25).

Persistence! Even our Lord demonstrated it by His life, by His very action. He did not give up until the miracle came!

Even the great apostle Paul believed in praying more than once. "Concerning this thing I pleaded with the Lord three times that it might depart from me" (2 Cor. 12:8). Paul didn't give up praying until the Lord showed him the answer. If Jesus didn't give up, and if Paul didn't give up, then we shouldn't give up. We should hang in there until the answer comes.

Jesus Persisted in Prayer at Gethsemane

Just before going to the cross, our Lord spent a night in prayer. He admonished His disciples,

"Watch and pray, lest you enter into temptation. The spirit indeed is willing, but the flesh is weak." He went away again a second time and prayed, saying, "O My Father, if this cup cannot pass away from Me unless I drink it, Your will be done." And He came and found them asleep again, for their eyes were heavy. So He left them, went away again, and prayed the third time, saying the same words (Matt. 26:41–44).

Jesus, our Lord and Savior, believed in praying more than once, saying the same words when He did so.

Throughout the Old and New Testaments, we have scores of illustrations of those who believed it necessary to hold on in prayer until the answer came, even if the matter must be presented to God several times.

Therefore, on the basis of biblical evidence, I urge you, my friends: don't give up in prayer. Don't give up.

My mother prayed for my father for seventeen years before the answer came. If anything is worth praying for, it's worth doing it right. Pray and pray again. Write down your request; write it on the wall of your room if necessary. But pray. Repeat your request. Repeat it with thanksgiving and praise to the Father. But repeat it.

And in His perfect timing our loving heavenly Father will give you what you need. You can count on it.

12

The Problem of Unanswered Prayer

Most of us have repeatedly heard that "God answers prayer" and "Prayer changes things." We print little signs and plaques to this effect and mount them on the walls of our homes and Sunday school rooms, and put bumper stickers with the same message on our cars. This is all well and good, because those statements are basically true.

But as wonderful and powerful as prayer is, and as much as God delights in answering the prayers of His children, the fact remains that there are times when our prayers seem to be unanswered. That can be very troubling, especially in light of what we know about God's pleasure in answering.

So we need to look at some of the reasons why prayers don't get answered. It is important that we be aware of those things that block our prayers. Then we can do something about them: we can remove the obstacles and begin to see the power of prayer flowing in our lives again.

Lack of a Close Relationship with God

We need to realize first that effective prayer grows out of a close relationship with God through Jesus Christ. God is always available to speak with us, and we need to develop the habit of meeting with Him regularly to discuss the concerns of our hearts and His. We need to commune with Him often, not just when we have a problem. Then, when we have a specific request or need for guidance, we are comfortable in His presence and attuned to hearing His voice when He answers.

Developing a relationship with God involves the reading and study of the Bible as well as prayer, of course, but prayer is simple and always available—you can pray at any time, in any place, and God is there to speak with you. Many people, however—even, amazingly, professing believers—simply do not pray at all. They may neglect prayer out of laziness or lack of love for the Lord or lack of appreciation for prayer's power. These are serious problems. But many do it simply on the false assumption that "God knows what my needs are, and He will just give me what I need. And since He's going to give me what I need anyway, there's no need for me to pray."

There are others who say, "Well, I'm just a housewife (or janitor or whatever), and I don't think God's too interested in a little nobody like me. He's busy with important people like Billy Graham. So I don't pray much."

Both of those attitudes are wrong. It is true that God knows what we need, but as our loving heavenly Father, He wants us to talk with Him and express our needs. First Peter 5:7 tells us to be constantly "casting all your care upon Him, for He cares for you."

The reason for this is our own good; we need to express our concerns to someone who cares. And God not only cares, but He is able to meet our needs. Thus we are told in Philippians 4:6: "Be anxious for nothing, but in everything by prayer and supplication, with thanksgiving, let your requests be made known to God."

When we obey this instruction and discuss our concerns with the Father, what will be the result? "And the peace of God, which surpasses all understanding, will guard your hearts and minds through Christ Jesus" (Phil. 4:7).

In the second case, shyness or feelings of inferiority are not viable reasons for anyone's failure to pray, because God is no respecter of persons—He doesn't play favorites. He will answer the prayer of a housewife or a queen, a mechanic or a king, a farmer or a sales clerk, a preacher or a businessperson. He wants to hear from you just as much as He wants to hear from Billy Graham, and He will listen as closely and lovingly to you as to anyone else.

There is another reason why an intimate relationship with God is crucial to seeing prayers answered. One of the conditions of prayer that God has given us in the Bible is that prayers He will answer must be prayers in line with His plans. First John 5:14 tells us, "Now this is the confidence that we have in Him, that if we ask anything according to His will, He hears us."

How do we discern the will of God so that we can be increasingly confident, as time goes by, that our prayers are in accord with His will? The answer, again, is to spend time with Him in His Word and in prayer so that our knowledge of and intimacy with Him deepen. As we come to better know our God and His ways, we will find that our prayers are answered more often because they reflect His desires more often.

We need to catch a vision of the majesty, the glory, the holiness and righteousness of God. We need to realize that whereas our view of a situation is limited to our terribly imperfect, mortal ability to understand, the Lord says, " 'As the heavens are higher than the earth,/So are My ways higher than your ways,/And My thoughts than your thoughts' " (Isa. 55:9). We cannot hope to have the Father's perfect knowledge of a given situation and we need to appreciate His superiority. As we grow in our knowledge of and love for Him, however, we will also grow in our ability to discern His will and to pray in accord with it.

It is easy, given our imperfect understanding, to make a request we think is all for the good but God knows is not the best plan. For example, suppose you are concerned about a neighbor who is an unemployed accountant. You may hear about a job opening with Company A that sounds perfect for your neighbor. So you tell him about it and then ask God to give him that job. However, God may know that there are circumstances at Company A that would make it very difficult for your neighbor to be happy or productive there, and He may want to direct him to an opening you know nothing about at Company B.

My point is simply that God's knowledge is complete and His ways are wonderful, whereas we are very limited in our understanding. Thus, on many occasions when our prayers seem not to be answered, the problem may be that we have not asked according to His will. But as we come to know God and His will better, we will find that our prayers are increasingly effective.

Wrong Attitude or Motives

Wrong motives will certainly prevent one's receiving answers to his prayers. For instance, to petition God for things merely to satisfy one's selfish desires is wrong, and God will not honor that kind of prayer. James spoke to that point in his epistle: "You ask and do not receive, because you ask amiss, that you may spend it on your pleasures" (4:3).

One's goals should glorify God. "Therefore, whether you eat or drink, or whatever you do, do all to the glory of God" (1 Cor. 10:31). If you live by the philosophy of those words, you will see your prayers answered. But if you are selfish, self-centered, or self-indulgent, your prayers will not be answered.

John Knox, the great Scottish Presbyterian preacher, gave us a fine example of praying selflessly. "Lord, give me Scotland, or I die," he said. His burning desire was to see his entire nation come to saving faith in Jesus. And Mary, Queen of Scots, testified to the efficacy of Knox's praying when she said, "I fear that man's prayers more than I fear all the armies of England and France."

Pride is another wrong motive that will cause a person's prayers not to be answered. Jesus told a story of two men who went to the temple in Jerusalem to pray, "one a Pharisee and the other a tax collector" (Luke 18:10). In today's terminology, the Pharisee could be compared to a very proper, morally upright believer who is very zealous to see God's law obeyed. He believed in the Torah, the written Word of God, and he lived by the Law and the Prophets.

The other man might be compared to an unchurched man, one who lived in violation of the laws and rules of the church. He probably had cheated the people from whom he collected taxes, demanding more than was necessary and pocketing the difference.

So they both came to the temple to pray. We know why

the Pharisee came: it was his habit to do so, and he did, three times every day. We don't know why the tax collector came to pray. Perhaps he was having personal or health difficulties. At any rate, he came to the temple too. Jesus said,

> "The *Pharisee* stood and prayed thus with himself, 'God, I thank You that I am not like other men—extortioners, unjust, adulterers, *or even as this tax collector.* I fast twice a week; I give tithes of all that I possess.' And the *tax collector*, standing afar off, would not so much as raise his eyes to heaven, but beat his breast, saying, 'God be merciful to me a sinner!' " (Luke 18:11–13).

Which of these two men do you think was justified? Which one had his prayer answered?

Jesus gave us the answer. The Pharisee, who exalted himself, would "be abased" (v.14), or, in this case, not get through to God. But of the tax collector, who had humbled himself before God, Jesus said, "he... will be exalted" (v.14). The Pharisee prayed wrongly, with the wrong attitude. His prayer was denied. The tax collector prayed rightly. His prayer was answered. He went home a changed man, a new creature, by the power of almighty God.

Yes, there are some prayers that cannot be answered. They are prayed by the wrong people, with a wrong attitude, at the wrong time.

A person who is not fully committed to God and who prays with mixed motives will likewise see few prayers answered. An example here is the rich young ruler who came to Jesus seeking eternal life. Jesus saw the man's heart and knew that he loved his riches, his home, and his fast, carefree life more than he loved God. Jesus told him to sell all his possessions and give them to the poor.

"And come, follow Me" (Luke 18:22).

But, because of his riches, his security, and his selfishness, the man said, "I can't do it. I don't want to follow you to that extent." And the Bible tells us that the young man sorrowfully walked away from eternal life, because he was unwilling to free his heart of the sin of selfishness.

His love for money separated him from God.

A man doesn't have to be wealthy to hold back from God. Even a little money can hinder a man's serving God. And when money stands between a man and God, he cannot get his prayers answered.

I have had friends tell me that God said to them, "Give a thousand dollars to Lester Sumrall's ministry," but even though they had it, they refused to give. Later God spoke to them and said, "Make that two thousand." Again, though they had the two thousand, they refused to give. Later God upped the amount and told them, "Make it three thousand."

The principle involved has nothing to do with my particular ministry, whether they were to give a thousand or even three thousand dollars to the work I am doing. Instead, the principle has to do with the matter of a man's releasing the money that has him so bound up that it is keeping him from serving God. It is only when a man opens his heart and his bank account—the totality of all that he is and possesses—that God can open the windows of heaven to him and pour out true riches upon him.

Other Hindrances to Answered Prayer

There are other hindrances to prayer, such as unconfessed sin. "If I regard iniquity in my heart,/The Lord will not hear [me]" (Ps. 66:18). If I see sin in my own heart and ignore it, God will not hear me, David said, thus stating an unequivocal biblical principle. Likewise, if God sees sin in my heart, my prayers will not be answered. "Behold, the LORD's hand is not shortened,/ That it cannot save;/Nor his ear heavy,/That it cannot hear./But your iniquities have separated you from your God;/And *your sins* have hidden His face from you,/So that He will not hear" (Isa. 59:1–2).

If there is strife between a husband and wife, the husband's prayers will not be answered. "Likewise, you husbands, dwell with them [wives] with understanding, giving honor to the wife, as to the weaker vessel, and as being heirs together of the grace of life, that your prayers may not be hindered" (1 Pet. 3:7). The same principle applies to the women. If they mistreat their husbands, their prayers will not be answered either. Where there is domestic tranquility, answers to prayer abound. But strife, bickering, cynicism, sarcasm, and general lack of peace in a home guarantee that prayers will not be answered.

Idolatry of any kind is also a hindrance to prayer. " 'Son of man, these men have set up their idols in their hearts, and put before them that which causes them to stumble into iniquity. Should I let Myself be inquired of *at all* by them?' " (Ezek. 14:3). And the implied answer is an emphatic no!

Notice, though, God's placement of idols: "in their hearts" and "before them." What we think about and what we love to feast our eyes upon become idols. And idols prevent God's hearing our prayers.

An unforgiving spirit also prevents answered prayer.

If anyone has slandered or spoken evil of you, disappointed you, or if he has actually done you physical or financial harm, you must forgive him. Because, if you do not forgive, you will actually prevent your own prayers from being heard. A bad spirit renders prayer completely ineffective. " 'And whenever you stand praying, if you have anything against anyone, forgive him, *that your Father in heaven may also forgive you* your trespasses' " (Mark 11:25).

Being inconsiderate of the poor hinders prayers. "Whoever shuts his ears to the cry of the poor/ Will also cry himself and not be heard" (Prov. 21:13). Generosity and Christian victory go hand in hand. Much prayer is unnoticed and unanswered for the simple reason that we are deaf to the cries of human need. Hardness of our hearts stops God's giving to us.

Delay Is Not Denial

Finally, we need to bear in mind that dealing with delayed answers to prayers is one of the greatest problems concerning prayer. We have all experienced delayed answers to prayer. If you are impatient and expect or demand an immediate answer to your prayer, a delay *might seem* a denial, when an hour, a day, or a month later will prove you wrong. God answered your prayer, though not at the exact moment you uttered the petition.

An example of this is to be found in John's writings. Mary and Martha's brother was very ill, and the sisters prayed that their brother's health would be restored. Despite their prayers, Lazarus died and was placed in a tomb. Certainly, to the sisters and friends of Lazarus, it appeared that their prayers had been to no avail. Days later, when Jesus spoke the words of resurrection power, they realized that their prayers had not been denied; the answer was merely postponed.

If you have been praying for a situation and the answer has not come immediately, please don't give up in discouragement. If you have been living right and praying right, your prayers will be answered. You can count on it.

Ten lepers came to Jesus, begging, praying to be healed. Though He spoke words of encouragement to them, they were not immediately healed. But as they obeyed Him they were healed. Again, delay was not a denial. Their earnest prayer was answered. Read the account in Luke 17.

"And behold, a woman of Canaan...cried out to Him, saying, 'Have mercy on me, O Lord, Son of David! My daughter is severely demon-possessed' " (Matt. 15:22). A worried mother wept and prayed that Jesus would heal her daughter. But Jesus seemed not to hear her.

Undaunted, the woman worshiped Him and sought Him again. The disciples, wearied with her entreaties, wanted to send her away. But the woman persisted, and her request was granted—not a denial, only a delay.

My friend, if your earnest prayer seems not to have been answered, if your healing is not complete, if your need is not completely met, don't become discouraged. Don't give up. If you are living right and praying right, you are experiencing only a delay, not a denial!

13

For Whom and for What Should We Pray?

It is no surprise that human beings have a tendency to be selfish and self-centered in their prayers—to "ask amiss," as James 4:3 puts it. But as we saw in the last chapter, God will not honor such prayers, and that is only right.

The Bible doesn't merely tell us, however, that improper prayers will not be answered. It also gives us clear instruction in what people and things we *should* pray for. An old Southern preacher once said, "There are two basic kinds of prayer: shotgun prayers and rifle prayers. When you pray shotgun prayers, you just pray in some general direction, hoping you'll hit a target. With the rifle prayers, you take careful aim and shoot, knowing you have a specific target in mind, and knowing that your prayers will accomplish their desired end."

So if we want to pray and receive answers to our prayers, we must give proper attention to this very important matter of "targeting our prayers," so as to prevent the possibility of praying amiss.

For Whom Should We Pray?

Not necessarily in exact order of importance (for they are all important), there are a number of people and groups of people for whom we should be concerned enough to pray.

1. *We should pray for our families.* These people are

our prime responsibility. We cannot, we dare not, overlook them. We must pray for our parents. We should pray for our children. We should pray for other relatives who are living with us. We should pray for those who are miles away, either in schools or jobs.

Abraham prayed for his family. He prayed that his wife would bear him a son. He prayed that God would supply a sacrifice in Isaac's stead. In fact, one of the prime reasons God chose Abraham to be the leader of his nation was because, "I have known him, in order that he may command his children and his household after him, that they keep the way of the LORD" (Gen. 18:19). God chose Abraham because He knew he would assume spiritual leadership of his family.

2. *We should pray for the salvation of all people everywhere.* "I exhort first of all that supplications, prayers, intercessions, and giving of thanks be made for all men" (1 Tim. 2:1).

John Knox prayed, "God, give me Scotland." David Livingstone prayed, "Give me Africa." Hudson Taylor prayed, "Give me China." All of these men had visions that went beyond their own limited borders. But perhaps John Wesley's encompassed them all, including his own, when he declared, "The world is my parish!"

If " 'God so loved *the world* that He gave His only begotten Son' " (John 3:16) for that world, then we ought to pray for that world. God said, " 'Ask of Me, and I will give You/The nations for Your inheritance,/And the ends of the earth for Your possession' " (Ps. 2:8).

3. *We should pray for our own city.* Though Jonah was not native to Nineveh, the city became "his" when "the word of the LORD came to Jonah the son of Amittai, saying, 'Arise, go to Nineveh, that great city, and cry out

against it; for their wickedness has come up before me' " (Jon. 1:1–2).

When Jonah eventually did as God commanded, multiplied thousands turned to God—all because one man obeyed the voice of God that spoke to him as he prayed.

Jesus prayed for Jerusalem: " 'O Jerusalem, Jerusalem, the one who kills the prophets and stones those who are sent to her! How often I wanted to gather your children together, as a hen gathers her chicks under her wings, but you were not willing!' " (Matt. 23:37).

Have you wept over your city? Have you prayed that your city's inhabitants would turn to the living God? Praying for our city is certainly within the scope of the plan that Jesus had in mind when He said, " 'You shall be witnesses to Me in Jerusalem' " (Acts 1:8). Personalize these words of Jesus by substituting the name of your own town or city.

4. *Pray for your nation.* Certainly America has become a great nation because of the prayers of those early settlers of our country. Even from the outset, the discovery of our land can be attributed to our heavenly Father. Christopher Columbus gave credit to God for directing him to this New World.

In his logbook he wrote, "It was the Lord who put into my mind (I could feel his hand upon me) the fact that it would be possible to sail from here to the Indies-....There is no question that the inspiration was from the Holy Spirit, because He comforted me with rays of marvelous inspiration from the Holy Scriptures."

Read any of the Old Testament prophets, and see how they yearned for their people, Israel, to return to God. In our own time, if ever a country needed prayer, America does. We should make it a matter of urgency to pray for our churches and schools, for our mothers and fathers, for our children. Pray that the children will be protected against the sin that is rampant in the schools and colleges. Have you been praying for your country?

5. *We should pray for protection from adversaries.* Jacob did: "Then Jacob said, 'O God of my father Abraham and God of my father Isaac,... Deliver me, I pray, from the hand of my brother, from the hand of Esau; for I fear him, lest he come and attack me and the mother with the children" (Gen. 32:9–11).

Moses prayed for victory over Israel's enemies. King David prayed for victory in the many battles he fought. We should pray for our great land. Pray that our land will have peace within its borders. Pray that our young men will not have to go to war. Pray that we will be protected against threatened nuclear holocaust.

6. *We should pray for the workers in Christ's service.* Many joke about the "soft" life ministers, evangelists, and missionaries have. My friend, please don't be guilty of such joking at the expense of your servants for Jesus' sake. I know of no more grueling, demanding service than that for our King. God is not a hard taskmaster, but those who are in earnest about the Kingdom realize that their task can never be finished.

Often these great men and women work too hard, for too many long hours, and literally burn themselves out for the gospel. And why do they do it? Because there is no one to stand in the gap to help them.

Pray for your pastors. Pray for your evangelists. Pray for your missionaries. Pray for your church officers. Pray for your Sunday school teachers. Pray that more help will come so that they can more effectively share the good news. "Then He said to His disciples, 'The harvest truly is plentiful, but the laborers are few. Therefore pray the Lord of the harvest to send out laborers into His harvest' " (Matt. 9:37–38). Pray for all who are involved in spreading the gospel of the Kingdom. Help them carry their tremendous load.

7. *We should pray for the leaders of our land.* "Prayers, intercessions, and giving of thanks, [should] be made for...kings and all who are in authority, that we may lead a quiet and peaceable life in all godliness and reverence" (1 Tim. 2:1–2).

If ever a man needed someone to pray for him, our president does. Even though he has some of the very best counsel possible to obtain, and even though he delegates thousands of important decisions, the really big decisions are his alone. President Harry Truman said it well when he stated, "The buck stops here." Pray for our president.

Pray also for judges and other law-making and law-enforcing bodies and individuals. Pray for governors, mayors of cities, and legislators. Pray daily for these and other individuals in authority by name. We can change our nation by our prayers.

For What Should We Pray

We have many biblical examples of what God's people have prayed for. Perhaps by taking a closer look at these godly people and their effective prayers, we can get an idea of the wide spectrum of things and situations for which they prayed and thus generate more faith to receive for our own praying. The list is long and varied, but in these few pages the following illustrations will provide a sort of spot check to show us the kinds of prayers that God has answered for His people.

1. *You can pray for the physical needs of life.* For example, water is an absolute necessity of life. People can live a lot longer without food than they can without water. And when the people of Israel followed Moses out of Egypt and into the Sinai desert, they faced several situations where they did not have water fit to drink. On such occasions, Moses took the problem to God. We see one of these in Exodus 15, where the people came to a place of bitter, undrinkable water and Moses "cried out to the LORD, and the LORD showed him a tree; and when he cast it into the waters, the waters were made sweet" (v. 25).

God doesn't always do miracles in response to the physical needs of His people, but He promises to provide for them one way or another if we seek first His kingdom (see Matt. 6:33), and He invites us to pray about them.

2. As King Hezekiah did, *You can pray for physical healing.* This incident, too, was covered in a previous chapter. The king was very ill and God had told him he was about to die. But King Hezekiah turned his face to the wall and prayed. When he did, God said, " 'I have heard your prayer...and I will add to your days fifteen years' " (2 Kings 20:5–6).

Our all-powerful Lord is able to heal any ailment, and He invites you to pray for the health needs of yourself and others in accordance with His Word and will.

3. *You can pray that God will assist you in your family affairs.* Zacharias, the priest, and his wife, both of them elderly, desired a child. So they prayed and an "angel said to him, 'Do not be afraid, Zacharias, for your prayer is heard' " (Luke 1:13). I personally know of a

number of couples in a like situation, some of them young, and some older, who have asked God for a child, and He has given them one.

4. *You can pray for demons to depart.* Jesus did. "For He said to him, 'Come out of the man, unclean spirit!' Then He asked him, 'What is your name?' And he answered, saying, 'My name is Legion; for we are many' " (Mark 5:8–9). God answered Jesus' prayer, and He will do the same for us when we pray it with the same authority and power.

Many people are fearful of casting out demons. But it's not difficult. All you have to do is to say, "Lord Jesus, You are the captain of my salvation. And You have all power. You've got more power than this demon. So, in Your name, I command that demon to depart and this person to be set free!" If you are living for God in every dimension of your life, you can pray such a prayer in confidence in a loud voice, and the demon will have to go.

5. *You can pray that God will send spiritual assistance.* Cornelius was a Roman army officer who was seeking God. When Peter came to him in response to a vision, "Cornelius said, 'Four days ago I was fasting until this hour; and at the ninth hour I prayed in my house, and behold, a man stood before me in bright clothing, and said, "Cornelius, your prayer has been heard" ' " (Acts 10:30–31).

I know of numerous occasions when God heard the cry of a hungry heart by sending spiritual assistance. If you are crying out to God, be assured that He will send someone to you who will be able to show you the way to Him.

6. *No matter what your need, you can call upon God.*

When David was a shepherd boy, he often spoke to the Lord as he herded his sheep. And even later, when he became king, he continued to bring his needs to his heavenly Father: " 'I waited patiently for the Lord;/And He inclined to me,/And heard my cry' " (Ps. 40:1).

No matter who you are; no matter what your need; no matter if your concern is for yourself, another person, or a situation, God's Word plainly shows us that He will always meet the needs of His children. He said,

> 'Ho! everyone who thirsts [spiritual thirst],/Come to the waters;/And you who have no money [spiritually bankrupt],/Come, buy and eat./Yes, come, buy wine and milk/Without money and without price [I will provide for you, God is saying.]....Seek the Lord while He may be found,/Call upon Him while He is near' (Isa. 55:1,6).

Come to Him. Thrust yourself into His loving arms. He will show you how to pray, for whom and for what to pray, and He will satisfy the longing in your heart.

14

How God Has Answered My Personal Prayers

This chapter is the most intimate in the whole book. In it I open my heart and show you what's inside. I show you how I have often cried unto the Lord, and how He has met me right where I was at the time. I believe that the best Scripture I could use as a basis for these pages is one I have read, quoted, and believed more times than I can count. It is very, very true in my life, and, in all likelihood, is true in your life as well.

The words come from David, but they are universally true. "This poor man cried out, and the LORD heard him,/And saved him out of all his troubles" (Ps. 34:6).

My Mother Taught Me to Pray

My mother was a living example of prayer. She was a walking prayer, a veritable prayer in human flesh. I knelt before her knees when I was very small and she told me the words to pray, and I prayed them. She taught me my nighttime prayers, "Now I lay me down to sleep..." She taught me to say, "Thank You, Jesus, for the food."

My mother lived eighty-seven years, and in all my life I never heard her curse or blaspheme. Her mouth, as well as her heart, was clean before the Lord. What a treasure my mother was! She started me out on the road to God and heaven by her words, by her example, and by her godly teaching. I can never thank God enough for the mother He gave to me.

My First Real Prayers

Like most boys I prayed when I got in trouble. I made God all sorts of promises. But when the difficulty was past, I often forgot the promises. So I really doubt the deep sincerity of some of those early prayers.

But there came a day when I got serious with my praying. As a young man I contracted tuberculosis. I was very ill. My weight dropped to ninety-three pounds. I was literally skin and bones, unable to walk. For five months I was confined to bed. I was spitting up blood and getting continually worse.

Though I had been prayed for, those prayers didn't work, and it was clear to all that I was dying.

I realized my situation was desperate. So one night I got serious with God. I said, "Lord, if you will heal me of this terrible disease that's taking my life, I will preach for You."

And God healed me that very night! I never spit blood anymore. I was healed. Praise the Lord, I was healed! From that dramatic moment, my life was changed. I knew that God would continue to answer my prayers. He had just brought me from death to life. "This poor man cried out, and the LORD heard him" (Ps. 34:6).

My Search for Howard Carter

My sister and I were involved in evangelistic work when I had an opportunity to travel around the world with Howard Carter, an outstanding man of God. He was an Englishman, twice my age, but willing for me to go with him. But there was a problem: I had to catch up with him. By the time I had sold my car, obtained my passport, and made arrangements to go, he had gone to another country. Now, he didn't know how to reach me, and I didn't know how to get in contact with him.

When I asked his friends where he was, I got a number of different answers. One said, "Howard is in the Orient. Japan, I think. Or maybe it's China..."

Another said, "He's in India."

"I think he's in Indonesia," a third one told me.

All of this was totally baffling. What could I do? I went to the Lord in prayer. I said, "Lord, this man can't be all over the world at one time. Where is he? Please help me to find him."

The Lord spoke to my heart and impressed me with this idea, "Start from the bottom and work up."

I said, "I'll do it." So I purchased a ticket to Australia and New Zealand, looking for a man who was reported to be in Japan or someplace else in the Orient.

Once when I told this story, my listener said, "I wouldn't have done that."

"You would have if you had prayed," I answered him.

So I got on the boat and we sailed. We went to Suva and Tonga, then on to New Zealand. I was praying every day, "Lord, if I am to have a companion to go around the world with, please help me to find him!"

When we landed in Wellington, New Zealand, I prayed, "Lord, what do I do now?"

The Lord answered, "Go look for a certain church."

When I found the church, the pastor met me at the door. I said, "Sir, my name is Lester Sumrall. I'm from America, and I'm looking for a man named Howard Carter. Have you heard about him?"

The man stared. "Lester Sumrall! Yes, I know Howard Carter. I spoke to him just this morning by telephone."

"You did? Where is he?"

"Howard is in a prayer retreat way back in the mountains. But yesterday the most wonderful thing happened. The Holy Spirit told Howard that your ship was in the harbor, and that you would be looking for this church today."

Now it was my turn to be amazed.

The pastor continued, "Howard told me to come right down to the church to meet you, and to tell you that he would meet you in Australia in about three or four weeks."

You can see why I believe in prayer.

Howard Carter and I finally hooked up. Howard was a very precise, rigid Englishman, and we had agreed that we would never talk about finances. He never asked me how much money I had, and I never asked him how much money he had. Each of us always bought his own tickets and made his own travel arrangements. We had ministered together for a time when my money ran out. We were in Hong Kong at the time and were making plans to go to Tibet.

He said, "I think I'll go get my ticket and make my travel arrangements."

I said, "You go ahead. I'll take care of mine a little later." Howard may have wondered about my financial situation at the time, but he didn't say anything. Before he went to the ticket office, however, he said, "I'll tell you what. I'll book both of our tickets and tell them you'll be in to pick yours up later." I agreed.

So he went. I stayed in our room and prayed.

One night a short time later, while I was ministering there in Hong Kong, a Chinese lady came up for prayer. She looked and was dressed differently from the other

Chinese ladies, but I didn't think much about it. However, when she walked into the church the next night with three servants, all of them carrying huge boxes of canned fruit from California, I knew there was definitely something different about her!

I said, "What's all this?"

She smiled. "You are going to Tibet to minister. And you're going to need lots of canned fruit when you get there or you'll die. You couldn't eat their food."

"Thank you," I said, "but I don't have a ticket to go to Tibet yet."

She said, "You don't know me. I am the wife of a Chinese army general. I came all the way from China for an operation which was going to cost a lot of money. But last night when you prayed for me, the Lord healed me. Now I don't need an operation. And the Lord told me to give you the operation money." And she thrust a package into my hands.

I thanked her, thinking she might have given me one or two hundred dollars at the most. But when I opened the package in my hotel room, I was aghast. The envelope was stuffed with American fifty- and hundred-dollar bills. I had never seen so much money in my life!

The Lord spoke to me and said, "Now, go get your ticket to Tibet." I did so hastily.

The money that Chinese woman gave me bought me a boat ticket into Indochina, clear down to Hanoi. Then it bought me a ticket on a French railroad into the Hunan Province. There it paid for a horse and a man to care for him. I rode that horse through the hills for three months while we preached and ministered in Tibet. Then that Chinese lady's "operation money" paid my fare back to Hong Kong, with some left over. My friends, that's what God does for His children when they pray!

Led by Prayer in China

The adventures we had in China would fill a book in themselves. Many of them stand out, but none more than the time we got lost. We were traveling by mule team to our appointed place of ministry. When we left a small village, we saw not one road, but several, leading away. We had no idea which one we were to take.

We were lost in the middle of a remote inland Chinese town. What should we do? You guessed it. We prayed. And God sent us an angel. (At least, I will always believe that that English-speaking Chinese young man was sent to us from the Lord.)

This young man saw us pondering which road to take, and he approached us. "May I be of service?" he asked.

We were startled at God's quick response to our prayer. Here in the middle of China was a young Chinese man, addressing us in flawless English.

"Yes," I said, "we're lost. We don't know which of these roads to take."

After he had pointed us in the right direction, he told us, "Now I know why I came to this village. I had no reason for being here, but something led me here."

I told him that that "something" was the Lord.

While I was in China I bought a pair of shoes. The Chinese salesman smiled and assured me, "The shoes will be a ninety-five percent fit."

The man was right. But they were also a "five percent nonfit!" And that was horrible. I wore those shoes all the way through Japan, and Manchuria, and Mongolia. I wore them across Siberia and Russia, and Poland and

Germany, and Sweden and Finland. By the time I got to England, my feet were in terrible condition. I knew I had to do something about those shoes.

I also knew I needed money to take me back home. So I did what I was accustomed to do: I prayed.

Brother Carter and I had completed our tour and were no longer traveling together. By now I was a celebrity—a returned missionary! I was preaching at a different church almost every night. When I arrived at one church to minister, a lady handed me a parcel. "It's for you," she said.

I said, "I wonder who knew I'd be coming here?" I hardly knew that myself. I thought somebody had sent me some fruit or some food. But when I opened the package, what do you think it was? A pair of shoes.

"I'll try them on," I said. When I slipped my foot into the left shoe, it fit perfectly. I didn't even know my own shoe size; how could anybody else know it? "Praise the Lord!" I said. "I prayed for shoes, and here they are." God had laid it on somebody's heart to send me shoes—and in exactly the right size.

"Lord, that's better than I could even imagine," I said. Then I slipped my foot into the second shoe, but it wouldn't go in. There was something in the way. When I reached in to pull it out, I discovered a bundle of English pound notes! There was enough money there to pay my way to Canada and from there all the way home.

Later, when I told Howard Carter about the incident, he said, "But who knew your shoe size?"

"I have no idea," I said. And I never did find out who sent those shoes. It was a strange, beautiful thing about the way those shoes fit me, because English shoes and American shoes are built on a different last. Despite that, they fit me. Are you beginning to see what kind of a miracle life I have lived?

Led to Win a Million Souls

When God brought me back from the Orient, He told me, "Lester Sumrall, I want you to win a million souls."

I said, "Lord, how can I see that come to pass?"

He told me, "Get on television."

I'll admit I was fearful, so I started with a little radio station. It was successful. One day I met a man in Washington, D.C., who asked me, "Do you want a TV station?"

"Yes, sir."

"Well, I've got one for sale in Indianapolis."

"I'd buy it, but I don't have even ten dollars to spare."

In a total miracle transaction, he sold me the station for a million dollars, when I didn't have any money. But I signed for it on faith. Within a week, through a number of extraordinary transactions, even the amount owed was cut in half. The purchase of our South Bend, Indiana, station was as miraculous as the first one. Through the miracle action of prayer, I went on the air to reach and win the million people for Christ that God desired of me.

Our church in South Bend was expanding and we needed a building lot. I found just what we needed, but the asking price was forty-five thousand dollars. After praying about the transaction, I offered to buy the lot for thirty-five thousand dollars, with ten thousand down. The offer was accepted. But the best part of the deal was yet to come. I was able to sell a hundred-foot strip of the property for twenty-nine thousand dollars. That transaction left us with a prime piece of land that was just what we needed. And it had cost us only six thousand dollars. The acquisition was certainly a tribute to answered prayer!

My Wife's Healing

On our first missionary trip to Puerto Rico, my wife contracted malaria. When I consulted a doctor about her condition, he listened to me patiently and told me, "Reverend Sumrall, I'll be honest with you. Americans don't often survive malaria in our country. Your wife could be dead by the time you return home."

I was committed to preaching that evening, and I wept and prayed during the thirty-minute bus ride to the church. Over and over I heard the doctor's words, "Your wife may die...your wife may die..." I reminded the Lord that we had come to Puerto Rico to tell people about the saving, healing power of Jesus Christ.

When I stood up to preach, I said, "The doctor says my wife is dying." I raised my hands and said, "Lord, we came to Puerto Rico because You told us to come. We are Your faithful servants. So, right now, in the name of Jesus, I ask You to heal her. I thank You for healing her."

When I arrived home, her fever was gone! And even though we have spent weeks in malaria country since then, my wife has never had another attack of malaria. My friends, our God is faithful in answering the prayers of His saints!

My life has been a life of miracles wrought by prayer! And in this short chapter I've had time and space to tell you of only a few. There have been scores, even hundreds, of times when God came to our rescue or healed in response to our prayers. He provided finances when we prayed. He provided ways and means for ministry when we prayed.

The Secrets of Answered Prayer

You can understand by now that there are no true "secrets" to answered prayer. There are only principles that have not been learned.

You can also understand that any child of God can discover those secrets and can see his prayers answered. My mother before me discovered those secrets and taught them to me. I have learned those secrets, and this chapter has delineated some of the miracles God has performed in response to my prayers.

Therefore, since we are surrounded by a great cloud of witnesses to the power of prayer, I urge you to learn and apply these principles in your life. In ways that you may not have done it before, place your trust in the One who is the Master of the universe. Discover what He says about His power in your life, your body, and your circumstances.

Then, "Pray without ceasing." God will do the rest. He does everything well. Praise His name!